Tying and Fishing
the Fuzzy Nymphs

Tying and Fishing the Fuzzy Nymphs

by E. H. "Polly" Rosborough

Fourth Edition, Revised, Updated, and Enlarged
Foreword by Ted Trueblood

Stackpole Books

Copyright © 1988 by E. H. Rosborough
First Edition © 1965 by E. H. Rosborough
Second Edition © 1969 by the Orvis Company, Inc.
Third Edition © 1978 by E. H. Rosborough

Published by
STACKPOLE BOOKS
Cameron and Kelker Streets
P.O. Box 1831
Harrisburg, PA 17105

All rights reserved, including the right to reproduce this book or portions thereof in any form or by any means, electronic or mechanical, including photocopying, recording, or by any information storage and retrieval system, without permission in writing from the publisher. All inquiries should be addressed to Stackpole Books, Cameron and Kelker Streets, P.O. Box 1831, Harrisburg, Pennsylvania 17105.

Printed in the United States of America

10   9   8   7   6   5   4   3   2

Regular edition jacket design by Art Unlimited.
Book design by Art Unlimited.
Line art by Debbie Bond.

Library of Congress Cataloging-in-Publication Data

Rosborough, E. H.
   Tying and fishing the fuzzy nymphs.

   Includes index.
   1. Fly tying.   2. Flies, Artificial.   3. Nymphs (Insects)   4. Fly fishing.   I. Title.
SH451.R6   1988   688.7′912   88-2190
ISBN 0-8117-1818-2

Contents

Foreword by Ted Trueblood	7
Introduction	9
1. Discovery of the Fuzzy Nymphs	12
2. Preparing Materials for the Fuzzy Nymphs	34
3. Stoneflies	48
4. Caddisflies	70
5. Damselflies	86
6. Mayflies	90
7. Midges	124
8. Freshwater Shrimp and Scuds	132
9. Food Nymphs	140
10. Ideas and Theories	152
11. Equipment and Methods of Presentation	156
Afterword	181
Index	187

Foreword

The word "nymph" is used rather loosely by anglers to include both the aquatic form of various stream insects and the artificial flies that suggest or imitate them. We even include freshwater shrimp, or scuds, which aren't insects at all of course, but crustaceans.

The nymphs of which E. H. "Polly" Rosborough writes are those made with dubbing (spun fur) bodies. Year in and year out, cold weather and hot, high water and low, I think they are the most consistent trout catchers of all. Yet far too many anglers hesitate to fish any nymph because they fear it is too difficult, or else they can't find the types and patterns that catch fish. Both problems are solved in the pages that follow.

Compared to other forms of fly fishing, the use of artificial nymphs is fairly new. Polly Rosborough has been a pioneer in their development. He has devoted more than thirty years to this study, both in tying and use, and as a result he is well qualified to speak with authority on the subject.

This book was written for both the fly tyer and the angler. It tells the tyer, either amateur or professional, how to make nymphs that catch fish. It tells the angler how to use them. It should have been written thirty years ago, and it would have answered many of my own questions if it had been. This was impossible, obviously, because neither Polly nor anyone else then knew the secrets revealed in it. We are fortunate to have it now.

Ted Trueblood

Introduction

The introduction to the third edition of *Tying and Fishing the Fuzzy Nymphs* started out this way: "As an old popular song put it, 'There's gonna be some changes made.'" That theme will be carried on in this, the fourth edition.

Although the major change will take place all in one chapter, the one about the Golden Stone, there will also be a rather lengthy addendum at the end. This will encompass new theories, new methods, and include a lengthy dissertation on new materials and their uses. There will be a bit more Latin because there has been some taxonomic reclassification of the Golden Stone.

Actually, I couldn't care less about all the Latin references, but I find that more and more of late years one keeps meeting, shall we say, "erudite" fishermen, and nowhere is this more evident than among a group of "nymphers." When a bunch of these addicts congregate, especially if during the Happy Hour, you can expect anything, particularly when they are about to call for one for the road.

I well remember my first introduction to Charlie Brooks, which came about in just this way. Time: 1975; place: West Yellowstone, Montana. Exact time: the Happy Hour, across the street from the convention complex. A friend had invited me over to the bar for a drink before the President's Banquet later that evening. There were four of us at the bar, my friend and I and Charlie and a friend of his. They were engaged in a debate that I could see would never be resolved without some help from outside, so at what seemed an opportune moment I slipped into the conversation.

A natural "Buttinsky," you bet. Sometimes that's the only way to learn things, or gain a new friend. After a few passes back and forth, Charlie knew I was plenty smart on the subject in question and he exploded. "Say! Just who the hell are you anyway?" "Only Polly Rosborough," I answered. "Ought to have known it," he said. "No one else would have come up with your answers." And so a new friendship was born, and still endures. And it all started with a drink and an argument over the pros and cons of a couple of bugs.

In the following pages of this book, five scientific orders are discussed. After one short chapter on the Muskrat Nymph, which, as a rule, emerges as one of the Diptera, we find the five orders as follows:

Stoneflies: Order Plecoptera
Caddisflies: Order Trichoptera
Damselflies: Order Odonata, suborder Zygoptera
Mayflies: Order Ephemeroptera
Two-winged Midges: Order Diptera

These orders will be further broken down into various families and genera throughout the text, but in no case am I going to be caught out on an entomological limb, so to speak, expounding on some insect with which I am not on good speaking terms.

The first edition of this book covered a selection of fifteen nymphs. The second edition was expanded to cover twenty patterns, and the third edition contained twenty-five. In this, the fourth edition, we will stay with the twenty-five, because if I can't take trout on at least one of these twenty-five, all my own originals, well, I'll hang up my rod.

The fourth edition will carry all the way through from the larva, pupa, and nymph to the emerged adult on at least eighteen of the twenty-five nymphs. "Why not all of them?" you may ask. Well, the balance of them are either suggestive or crustaceans, and have no terrestrial or winged life stage.

But the most conspicuous change is that, thanks to the wealth of new synthetic materials today (including yarns never intended for fly tying), my original body-material process of blending and felting natural furs to get the proper amount of "fuzzy" in my nymphs is not necessary to get a winning fly.

I will be the first to take shortcuts, as readers of previous editions will see. Some patterns, such as the Muskrat, still require the fur "noodle" to look right because I have found no yarn that quite satisfies me. I do note a new muskrat yarn now on the market and it could well be the final answer, but the price is outrageous. One large supplier lists it in the bulk section at $250 per cone. It does not list its yardage or weight, but just imagine how many Muskrat Nymphs you would have to tie to pay for even one cone. So I have decided that as long as I can buy large damaged skins direct from local trappers for one dollar or less, I can do without muskrat spun yarn.

Here is the full story of the Fuzzy Nymphs from their beginnings fifty years ago.

Discovery
of the Fuzzy Nymphs

1

Over the past several years, an incredible amount of material has appeared on the tying and fishing of the nymphs, the immature stage of aquatic insects. Some articles were devoted entirely to materials and dressing procedures, others dealt only with nymph fishing techniques, and there are still big gaps to be filled in on this subject, which is important to both fishers of nymphs and fly tyers.

The history of *Tying and Fishing the Fuzzy Nymphs* itself illustrates how far we have come in the study of nymphs and nymph fishing over the last few decades. The book has expanded from an eighty-eight-page paperback to a full book, and as I mentioned in the Introduction, this fourth edition will include the full life cycle of eighteen of the twenty-five nymphs I have originated over the past forty-five years, that is, the adult, and in some cases, wet patterns, for the original nymphs.

Ever since I caught my first trout on a fuzzy nymph pattern forty-five years ago, I have been experimenting almost continuously with these patterns. In retrospect, the first cast I made with a nymph instead of a dry fly on my leader was a turning point in my angling pursuits, and it gave me a new outlook toward fly tying in general. I'm still exploring this new direction at every opportunity. The actual result of that first cast was that I have become a confirmed nympher, tying and fishing. That's not to say I fish nymphs exclusively—far from it. I enjoy every aspect of the fly-fisher's art. But that first experience hooked me for life: fooling a wary trout with a nymph of my own design still offers me the greatest challenge on the stream. Most anglers will admit the same, even if somewhat reluctantly.

It all began innocently enough. During the early Depression years I was living in northern California on a small winding creek well populated with brown trout, a few weighing up to four pounds. Smart was not the word for them. Every one had a framed diploma and seemed to delight in thumbing his highly selective nose at the local anglers who tried to fool them with a fly.

My best flies for outwitting these fellows were a super-floating #10 Black Drake Mayfly during the June hatch, and later in the season a floating #8 Meadow Grasshopper. But there were many fishless days, especially during the early stages of the various fly hatches, when only fish of ten inches or less would rise to my dry offerings. The old lunkers were bulging everywhere for something seemingly much different. It was a mystery and no one had an answer for me.

I sensed that this strange behavior called for something entirely different in both methods and patterns. I decided to abandon dry flies altogether, although I had no clear idea what it was I wanted to offer the big fellows. Using some fly tyer's instinct, I decided to step back a pace and try to imitate the nymphs I had seen illustrated in some mail-order catalogs. Even though they had none of the appeal that dry flies have for anglers, it was obvious the trout were not so snobbish.

Except for the late Edward R. Hewitt's work on nymphs, little was available in print at that time, and I was not even aware of the existence of *A Trout And Salmon Fisherman,* so I was almost starting from scratch. Looking back on it now, I see it was a good thing I did not have Hewitt's books or I would probably be using the traditional methods still employed by the majority of present-day tyers, and still catching the traditional number of fish. Hewitt's work was fine and I studied it carefully in later years, but nymph-tying methods and available materials and proper presentation techniques were then in their infancy, so I enjoyed a free hand in my search for a new way to take fish with a fly.

Like a lot of amateurs of the late twenties and early thirties, I possessed the catalogs of the now-defunct Willmarth Company of Roosevelt, New York, and Paul Young of Detroit, Michigan. Willmarth supplied me with the first materials for the fuzzy nymphs, and Young's catalog showed pictures of nymphs that I tried to imitate.

The first material I used was seal hair. I bought one-eighth ounce each of blue dun and natural cream, and my first look at it almost convinced me I would never be able to tie it on a hook. The seal fur was so short—only a quarter of an inch long—and so slick one could hardly hold onto it. But I am a stubborn Scot and I had eighty cents invested in that quarter-ounce of fur, a considerable sum in 1932. I would find a way.

My first nymph was dressed on a regular-length shank and weight #8 wet-fly hook. I had never spun any kind of fly

body up to that date and neither had I seen anyone else do it, so you can imagine the quandary I was in. But being of an inventive nature, I spread out a couple of inches of the fur a quarter of an inch wide and gave it a thin coat of waterproof cement. When it reached the tacky stage I lifted it off with a thin knife blade and rolled it into a cylinder the size of a wooden matchstick. Both ends were slightly tapered while still tacky, and when the "noodle" was thoroughly dry, I tied the thinnest end in at the bend of the hook. (At this point it might be well to clarify the word *noodle:* It will always refer to the fur cylinder you prepare in advance for nymph building.)

On the first nymph I used the cream seal fur. I must have been directed in this when I think of the explosive results this nymph later brought. With the working silk half-hitched back of the eye, I grasped the loose end of the fur noodle in the hackle pliers and twisted it into as tight a rope as I could without breaking it. It was then wound tightly around the hook in a close spiral to form a naturally segmented body. Each time the pliers went around the hook it was necessary to twist them once clockwise, otherwise the noodle would unwind.

To finish this first nymph, I added a soft grizzly hackle wound on in front and then clipped, leaving about a dozen flues on the underside to simulate the legs. It didn't look like much, but as it turned out I had unknowingly created a fair simulation of a caddis larva, and even today this combination of color and materials would be hard to beat. I have since tried myriad other materials and evolved improved methods of dressing, but let me tell you, that first fuzzy nymph was a killer.

For several seasons past, a dozen or more big browns holding under a bank had been refusing my best offerings, so it was to their hideout I went to try out this scrubby-looking monstrosity. By some lucky chance I started off right on the first cast, and not by any change from my usual dry-fly tactics; old habits are not that easily broken.

Knowing there was a good fish under the overhanging bank on the opposite side of the creek, I simply flipped the nymph onto the far bank, gave it a twitch, and let it drop on the water, just as I often did fishing drys. It had hardly submerged when the water boiled and I was fast to an eighteen-inch brown, which after a most creditable fight I landed.

The fish ate it up, and I mean literally. An hour later all that was left of the nymph were a few streamers of seal fur and the legs. But I had landed five browns of one to three pounds, and I was keenly aware that here was a new and very exciting fly-fishing idea. Forty-five years later I am still exploring it.

My first presentation of a nymph to the fish was very unorthodox by modern nymphing standards. I did nothing the way it was supposed to be done. I didn't cast upstream on a slack line and allow the nymph to roll along the bottom of the stream. I did nothing right by the experts who had written about the subject, but I caught fish—lots of them over the next few years. And I spent a great deal of time asking myself, "Why does this or that happen?" "Why do I have this kind of steady success in a field with which I am not familiar?" "Can it be that the first nymph fishermen simply did not go far enough?" "As long as their initial methods caught fish, why look any further?" There had to be a reason, possibly a lot of reasons.

I tried every method of presentation imaginable, and under all conditions of water, season, time of day, and weather. The final summation of all my research added up to a few proven facts. The first is that during a hatch, the larger fish prefer nymphs, and most nymph patterns are deadliest when fished rather shallow. This is particularly true during

the early part of the hatch when the larger fish are bulging just subsurface. Only the little fellows are jumping for the few flying adult insects. At such times the fish do not sink back to deep water between rises. They seldom sink more than six inches below the surface. The nymphs come drifting to them on the current, or rise from under them and are taken just below the surface. This is why the fisherman will often see a splash but never see the fish. At this stage of the hatch, dry-fly purists who swear they are feeding dry will beat their brains out trying to match the hatch.

Actually the fish appear to be tailing when they suck in

the nymph an inch or so below the surface and their tails pop out as they go down. Believe me, a big rainbow can make a resounding splash when he takes a large stonefly nymph—sounds almost like a scared beaver when it dives—but this does not necessarily mean the fish has taken an insect on the surface or above it.

The exceptions to this observation are any form of aquatic life the fish feed on that does not become a winged insect, such as a shrimp or scud. These nymphs are better fished at various depths, from one foot deep to allowing the fly to roll along the bottom of the stream. Actually, you cannot classify these food forms as nymphs at all; they are crustaceans and spend their entire life cycles in the water, but a good simulation of them is still very effective in taking fish subsurface.

I do not mean to say that nymphs fished deep will not catch fish. Several of the twenty-five patterns of nymphs included for discussion in this book may be fished with good success at all depths. These will be dealt with separately, and at length, as we come to them. I was to learn how different each nymph pattern was as I applied my new tying discovery to imitating other insect species.

The following June I added another pattern, the Black Drake Nymph. Over the forty-five years since, this pattern

has proved to be the greatest and most consistent killer of all on the West Coast. It is a strictly seasonal pattern and its effectiveness is restricted to late May through early July. This would seem to be an overlong emergence period for any natural insect, and in fact its effectiveness never lasts over two weeks in any one area, but latitude and elevation make for different emergence times for different waters.

The first Black Drake Nymph had a body of blue-dun seal fur, blue-dun hackle tail, and owl's eyebrow legs. (These last feathers are now illegal in most states, so no further mention will be made of them. After searching every yarn shop, furrier, and millinery shop for forty-five years, I have found acceptable substitute materials for many of my original ties.)

Sometime during that same midsummer I was fishing a small lake about two miles from home, and while the fish there were very poor eating unless smoked, they were good fighters, and of course they could always be released. Browns up to five or six pounds were available, though the average fish landed was in the two-pound class. You seldom landed the big ones. A lot of hazards like islands of floating pond lilies and underwater moss accounted for losses of up to seventy-five percent of all fish hooked.

This was the day I made the acquaintance of the first Green Damsel Nymph. I had already tied fair imitations of the adult damselfly, but I had never seen the nymph, or even a picture of it, so my learning of its existence was a real discovery.

There were numerous damsels on the wing that day, but the fish ignored them. Still, the fish were bulging all over the surface of the lake. I had enough experience by this time to recognize the situation, but I did not know how to identify the nymph in question.

Finally, I lay down across the back seat of the boat with my face close to the water and waited. Almost at once I was rewarded. Swimming just under the surface was the answer to my problem—about an inch long, a medium olive-green color, with three small propelling flappers for a tail. It certainly was a tasty tidbit for a fish. I have since learned the flappers are the insect's gills, which double as sculling oars. Anyway, I grabbed it, transferred it to a safety-match box and headed for home and the fly vise. On arriving home, I found it had hatched into a pale green damsel, so a lot of questions were answered then and there.

I had to have another date with those big browns, so I dyed part of the cream seal's fur a light olive, tied a fuzzy pattern to match what I'd seen, and the next day, armed with a half dozen of the new nymphs, I was back at the lake. Until I lost the last nymph those old lunkers kept me a busy man. For every fish I landed I lost a nymph to the next one. Every fish managed to encase itself in a gallon or more of lilies, so a net was useless, and this hazard also sundered a lot of tippets. But I had fun. I was now convinced that the fuzzy-nymphs tying technique could be applied to almost any underwater fly with tangible results. It was like finding the philosopher's stone; I couldn't wait to find another insect to simulate with a fuzzy-nymph pattern and then fish it. I was off on a real fly-tying adventure.

I tried yarns and other natural materials of all kinds for body materials, but the only requirement the fish had was that the resulting body be fuzzy and, of course, match the natural insect in size, shape, and color. While all this is accepted wisdom for the tyer of today, to me then it had the newness and excitement of a gold strike or the discovery of a new feeder stream full of native browns.

Many more nymph patterns were added to my list in the next ten or twelve years, and each went through several evolutions before a final version was decided upon. I experimented continuously, even with proven patterns. Even today I hold that no version of a nymph is ever accepted as final, because no matter how well it performs, it can always be improved. That attitude has led to some interesting moments at the tying bench.

Sometime during 1945 or 1946 a revolution occurred in my tying or assembly technique, and like many discoveries, this change came about purely by necessity. A lot of fly-tying materials were almost unobtainable during the later years of World War II, including seal, and in the search for body material I had accumulated a lot of floss skeins in odd colors that had to be dyed. The first time I tried this the dozen or so skeins came out a tangled mess, knotted practically beyond use. But after I dumped them back into the rinse water they started to separate of themselves, and a bit of careful rotating made each skein tangle-free. A light dawned on me at that moment: if the floss would separate in this way, why wouldn't fur mat or felt if thoroughly spun in soapy water. This idea must be investigated at once!

I sheared the belly of a muskrat skin and dumped the fur into a pan of hot soap suds, then spun it with a finger for a couple of minutes, reversing the direction several times. The

Spinning the fur in soap suds.

fur was then poured into a fine-wire strainer and hot water run through it to remove the soap. I wrapped the fur in a paper towel and squeezed it as dry as possible, then spread it out on more toweling to dry. The end result was a well-matted or felted mass that now suggested possibilities far beyond anything I had been using. It had the same fuzzy quality that the seal's-fur noodle had, which seemed to be the key to the patterns' successes, and took far less time to prepare.

Washing the soap out of the fur in a fine-wire strainer.

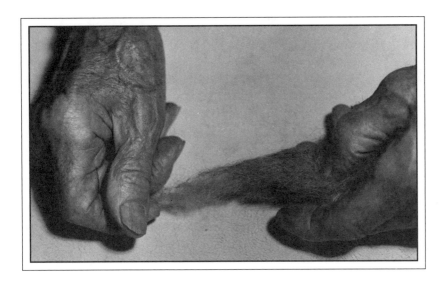

The fur teased out to make a "noodle."

Of late years I use the electric blender for making my dubbing, but only in small amounts or I wind up with a ball of rope wound tightly around the spindle. Put only a small handful of fur in the blender at one time. Fill it one-third full of hot water, add a tablespoon of soap flakes, put the lid on, and set the speed on 3 (my Hamilton Beach blender has seven speeds). It only takes a half minute for a thorough blend. Pour the mixture into the strainer and follow the preceding instructions for the final result. If you are blending several different furs or chopped-up synthetics, do not use more than ten-percent of fibers longer than three-quarters of an inch, or you will wind up with a rope, just the same as you would by overloading. A big dishpan is still best for producing large amounts of dubbing; I load mine with a quarter pound of fur at a time.

Producing The Noodle

Depending on the length and type of fur a tyer is using, he will find it will take a bit of time and practice to tease out just the right amount of felted fur for any given size nymph. A small wad of fur is best to work with and will produce a dozen noodles. Holding this small wad in one hand, use the thumb and forefinger of the other hand to tease out a very small amount at a time—never more than enough to pull it halfway apart. For a #8 hook the amount required is about two inches long and short of half an inch wide, also very thin. Now, dampen the tips of the middle and third fingers and roll the fur in the palm of the hand into a long cylindrical noodle. You will find it has probably lengthened a half inch or more, but you need this extra length for a #8 hook. Taper one end for one-half inch, the other half as much. You are now ready to tie a fuzzy nymph.

The Muskrat Nymph

The only reason for this nymph being considered first is because it came first when I started using the new felting process. It is also the easiest and fastest pattern to spin and allows for a good lucid explanation of all procedures. Actually, it should come much later in the book; the larva of one of the midges, Diptera, its family and genera will be dealt with more fully when we reach that section of the book.

The Muskrat Nymph really simulates the larval stage of both the gray cranefly and the black midge (both of which have light gray bodies and black heads), which accounts for the wide range of sizes in which this nymph can be tied—#8 to #16—to catch fish consistently.

Regarding the word "simulation": all the nymphs described in this book are simulations, never are they supposed to be true imitations. To be imitations they would have to be latex, plastic, or even rubber. Knowing in advance that devotees of the realistic school will be highly critical of my stand in this respect, I will state here and now that such nymphs catch many more unwary anglers than they do fish.

The Muskrat is the easiest of the full complement of twenty-five nymphs to tie when it comes to spinning the fur

The finished Muskrat Nymph.

noodle. Many of those dressed with yarn bodies are easier, but it is important that the original spinning technique be recorded first. Learning to spin natural materials allows the fly tyer a kind of self-sufficiency in creating body material.

Tying the Muskrat Nymph

Tying Thread: Bonded flat nylon, 00 or 000 in black. Formerly I used all Nymo but very little of this is now available so it is almost necessary to use Monocord or something similar.

Hook: This pattern, being most versatile, may be tied in sizes ranging from #6 to #16, and a 3XL Sproat bend is preferred. Use regular weight for shallow fishing and 2XS for deep or fast water.

Your fur noodle may be of various felted furs, or even blended of several different kinds, just so long as it is pale-to-medium gray. Since publication of the first edition of this book, I have done a lot of research into furs that can be used in the tying of nymphs, and I have finally reached the conclusion that all fur is grist for the mill: I use everything from poodle fur to mink.

Body: About the best possible felted fur for the Muskrat is muskrat belly, beaver belly, and jackrabbit back, with the guard hairs removed from the jackrabbit. Mix this thoroughly in proportions of two parts each of muskrat and beaver to one of jackrabbit. The main purpose of the jackrabbit is to act as a binder for the two shorter furs, thus strengthening the noodle.

Clamp the hook in the vise and coat it with heavy clear cement. Start the tying thread at the eye of the hook and wind tightly to the bend but not down on the curve, then half-hitch once.

Your noodle should be about two-and-one-half inches long (see Step 1) for a 3XL #10 hook, and thin—the diameter of a wooden kitchen match. Tie in with the tying thread the longest, thinnest tapered end at the bend of the hook. With this thin end tied in, make a couple more turns with the working thread. Catching the thread in a forefinger, pull out enough to make a loop a half inch longer than the noodle, then overwind it enough for the loop to be secure. Now wind the thread back toward the eye of the hook and half-hitch it

Step 1: A rolled noodle and a proper guinea hen feather for the legs of the Muskrat.

where you want the body to stop. On a #10 hook this will be about one-eighth inch. Put a heavy coat of cement on the hook and stretch out the loop and coat it also.

Now, unless you have been a pupil of mine, you are about to see a completely new departure from the usual techniques of fly tying: Catch the "out" end of the loop and the

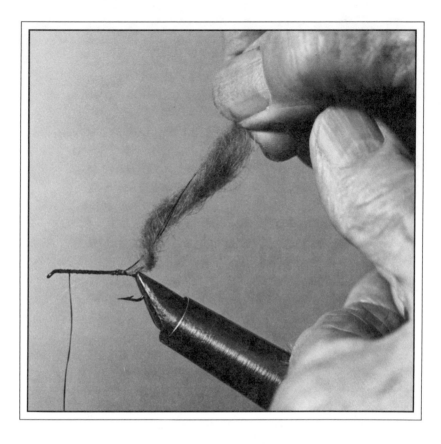

Step 2: Proper position of the spinning loop and noodle for spinning.

loose end of the noodle together, slide the noodle down alongside the loop (Step 2) enough so that when you start to twist them together the loop will be inside the twisted noodle and not visible. Twist or spin them up tight with fingers or hackle pliers as much as the thread will stand without breaking. The noodle should now look like Step 3.

Now, grasp the end in your hackle pliers and start winding it around the hook into the thick cement. For every time you make a turn, twist the hackle pliers a complete turn, otherwise the noodle will unwind. When making the last

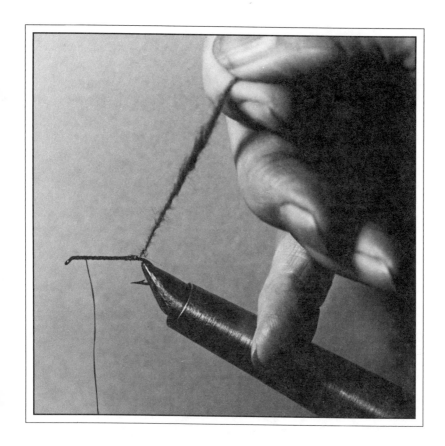

Step 3: The twisted noodle ready to wind.

turn, let it unwind enough so that when you tie it off it will flatten and make a neat front.

An important note here: Try to finish all bodies on top. This tends to eliminate lumps on the side of the bodies and heads. With practice in making noodles you eventually will make the last turn with not much left to tie off but the loop. Tie off with two half-hitches and cement it down. You now have a very durable fur body that can be roughed up quite a bit without danger of tearing the loop.

If you are curious by now about my seeming obsession

Step 4: The Muskrat Nymph body before scoring.

Step 5: The Muskrat body after scoring. The guinea legs are in place; I like to turn the fly upside down for this operation. Now wind in three ostrich flues for the head.

with half-hitches, here is an explanation! I never use a bobbin or thread holder of any kind but prefer to work directly from the spool. Not having the weight of the bobbin to hold the thread tight between operations, the half-hitches are a necessity; the added cement is always good insurance for durability.

Observe Step 4 carefully: the body is fuzzy, but not fuzzy enough, so it must be roughed up in some manner. In the past few years another tyer has come up with a top tool for this job. Break off three inches from either end of a hacksaw blade with a heavy pair of pliers; pick a blade with extra-fine teeth. Wrap the broken end with several turns of half-inch black rubber electrical tape and you have the best body scorer possible. Now score the top and sides, then turn the hook upside down and score the bottom.

With the hook upside down in the vise, tie in six or eight filaments of finely speckled guinea-hen body feather, or a comparable feather in a color (Step 5) such as teal or canvas-back duck. All of these feathers are good. These simulated legs should be one-quarter inch long for a #10 hook and centered on the underside, not spread out on each side (as they will be on the stone and mayfly nymphs). Finish off the head (Step 6) with three or four twisted strands of black ostrich flues. The ostrich head should be the same thickness as the front end of the body.

The final tie-off of two half-hitches should be placed right at the back of the head and underneath where it is not visible. Cut off the thread closely with fine-pointed scissors and give the head a coat of clear cement. Later, when it's dry, I use a second coat of jet black.

You have just tied your first fuzzy nymph. There's more to come.

Step 6: The finished Muskrat Nymph.

Preparing Materials for the Fuzzy Nymphs

2

When the first edition of this book was published in 1965, I was soundly berated by several friends for not including a chapter on preparing materials for fuzzy nymphs. Actually, I had very little excuse at that time. If the idea did occur to me, I probably did not think it was quite relevant to the general subject of tying and fishing nymphs.

However, since I am now in full-time production of the fuzzy nymphs, I find it necessary to come up with a lot of new procedures for dyeing, bleaching, and blending materials. Natural materials are not always available in desirable colors; this is especially true of the natural fur colors. Then again, if one wants to use the furs in natural colors only, it is a good idea to know how to blend different colors to obtain a heather mixture; even two or three colors of gray well mixed are far better than one.

The information in this chapter is meant to help the person who ties for his own use or, like myself, is a small commercial tyer. What got me into this phase of the trade was my desire for elusive colors of hackle that were not supplied by any fly-material outlet. I am not a technician or a professional dyer. I do not understand the kitchen chemistry involved in the processes that will follow here. I only know I eventually arrive at the desired end. This takes time and experiment if the color is unusual or the material is new to me, and this combination sometimes results in language never heard in Sunday School. But I seldom have to throw any material away due to ruining it. The only material I still have a problem with is Indian gamecock necks; when I tried bleaching fiery brown to ginger with twenty-volume hydrogen peroxide as the bleaching agent, I found that though I could eventually end up with a beautiful golden ginger, the center quill was totally brittle. I soon gave up on this idea. I then resorted to dying white or cream to ginger and I still do, even after I learned to mix the twenty-volume with Basic White booster powder. The necks still come out a bit brittle, though they can be wound without breaking after being soaked in hot water for a minute or two. Still, dyeing the white or cream is more satisfactory. My formula for ginger at present gives a bright golden ginger: Rit, one part yellow, one part tan, and one part gold. I always dye one or two feathers first, dry them, and if they're not right, add a bit more of the color needed.

Dyeing

Three common kitchen utensils are needed for proper dyeing. First, a straight-side cooking pot with a long handle (this should be enamelware; aluminum absorbs dye too much). When full, the pot should hold a gallon of water. You will need a french-frier screen that is one-half inch or more smaller than the pot and that, when suspended on its ears, its bottom should be at least an inch above the bottom of the pot. Direct contact is what ruins fine hackle; it actually leaves the flue with a curly, singed appearance. If you don't boil the dye, contact with the vessel's sides will not hurt the material, but this method is inferior to correct dyeing and sunlight and water soon fade the coloration.

You can dispense with the third utensil if desired, but it is handy. This is a handled fine-wire strainer to pour the material into and drain off the dye bath. If your french-fry screen has a long handle, simply lift material from the dye bath and run cold water through it till the water runs through clear.

Since the second edition of this book in 1969, the Rit company has introduced most of their dye colors in the new concentrated liquid form, a real boon to fly tyers. Gone is the need to follow our pursuit in the garage or woodshed, cleaning up the old finely powered dye, which required a lot of time to wipe up again and again, when we were sure we had gotten it the first time. So far, the purveyors of such sundries have not stocked quite all of the colors we need, but more and more are showing up on the store shelves, so eventually the full color chart will be available at your grocers.

Only all-purpose Rit will be discussed as a dyeing agent.

Formerly, I used Putnam's extensively, but it is so hard to find in recent years that I have set it aside. If you are lucky enough to find a good display of it, don't pass up any useful colors. You can use it the same as Rit. Just use one-third less in volume—it is very powerful. Two colors originally put out by Putnam that come to mind are irreplaceable: bronze-green and silver-gray green. I could certainly use some of the latter color for dyeing the immature stage of my Wet Green Damsel.

Years ago I was told you could not dye feathers or hair without first using a wetting-out agent called *Ferezal*. This was used to remove all the grease and natural oils from the material to be dyed so the dye could penetrate it. This is a lot of malarkey. If you remove the natural oils you also remove strength and gloss, leaving hackle, feathers, or hair dead and lifeless. Wash the material in a weak solution of hot soapy water, just enough soap to get the dirt or perhaps dried blood out. Too much soap and too long a bath tends toward the same results as when you use Ferezal.

Until you have gained some experience at dyeing you should never dump all the materials in the dye and hope for the best. Let's say you are going to dye some wood duck. One of the hardest colors to imitate is lemon-barred wood duck. Some twenty or more years ago I bought an ounce of dyed mallard from a big feather-supply house. It was so close in color to the real thing that I immediately ordered a half-pound to have a big supply of the same dye job. It took me years to use this up, but then I couldn't match it anywhere from various suppliers so the only answer was to dye my own. After repeated mixes of dye I finally settled on the following: two parts of tan Rit to one part of gold Rit. Make this mixture weak.

Take a natural lemon-barred feather and soak it well in hot water. It will darken at least a shade. Now take a large mallard side: hold the quill in a pair of long-nosed pliers and swish it around in the dye. Lift it out repeatedly and wash any excess dye out under cold water until its color matches the color of the real wood duck. If you find the mix does not give you the right color, pour off one-third of the water and add a bit more of the tan or gold, whichever is needed. Replace the water you poured off with fresh hot water. The idea is to keep the strength of the dye constant, otherwise you may get too much color and have to resort to lightening the material with No-Color Bleach, which works well on yarns, but can and does, for me at least, ruin some fine hackle.

Now start over with a fresh mallard feather. This time should do it; if so, dump the balance into the pot and start stirring. It seldom takes more than two minutes to dye mallard the lighter colors if the dye is boiling. The instant the feathers reach the color tone of the last sample take the french-frier screen out of the dye bath and run cold water through it till it runs out clear. It is always better to find the feathers need a bit more instead of less. Just return the material to the bath. Never match any wet material with dry for color.

There are certain colors that are badly distorted when viewed under an incandescent light bulb, in particular, anything with a purplish cast. It will always appear much browner than in sunlight. To counteract this, I check all colors under my fluorescent work lamp. This is a two-element, shaded, swivel-neck desk lamp and it has two tubes. One is soft white, the other is a daylight bulb. These cross fire with no flicker and no shadows. By careful checking this way I find that all colors I view under the light are identical when taken out into bright sunlight.

While you have your wood-duck dye all mixed, you might just as well dye up some ginger hackle. I tie a great many Light Caddis in sizes from #2 to #12, all bucktails for the local anglers. As a consequence, I use a lot of long ginger saddle. This is not always available, at least not long enough for palmering a #4 fly, but long white or cream is nearly always available, so I dye it.

I buy it strung and bundled and dye the whole bundle; that is, all but the butts, which I don't use. No use wasting your dye. Add enough gold Rit to the pot to make it about even with the amount of tan used. Find a natural ginger hackle you want to match in color. Get it thoroughly wet and you are ready.

It takes a bit longer for saddle hackle to dye than mallard, but seldom more than two to three minutes. If at any time you happen across some material that refuses to take dye fast enough, just throw a handful of plain table salt into the dye. This tends to set the color if it keeps washing out in the rinse water.

These strung and bundled saddles are always well cleaned and I find it unnecessary to prewash them. It might be a good idea to use the long-nosed pliers to hold and swish the bundle around in the dye. Otherwise it is too easy to scald your fingertips.

I must mention synthetics at this point. Some can be dyed, such as acrylic and mohair blends, but only the mohair dyes well, so the results will be guesswork. I dyed a ball of maroon blend with a whole package of purple and found I had the perfect answer for the bodies of my *Isonychia velma* nymph—maroon with a purple overlay; you might call it a heather, and such color combinations are always better than a solid color.

The true acrylics cannot be dyed, that is, unless you want to go to the trouble of using the commercial aniline dyes and do it under steam pressure. Take my word for it, it isn't worth the trouble.

Anyone who has ever tried doing a black dye job has probably had the same results I first had. Only the commercial aniline dyes will yield a true black, and as I said before, well, skip it. But a good dead black can be had with Rit simply by adding one-fourth part dark brown. Alone, black dyes a deep midnight blue and you can control the effect to an exact degree by the judicious addition of dark brown. Natural black feathers or hair are rarely a true black; hair will have a brownish tinge and hackle will be greenish. You can even match this last color by adding one-eighth as much dark green as black to your mixture.

Ostrich plumes are about the hardest feather to dye precisely. I use a lot of both natural and black ostrich in the tying of nymphs, and find that the large top-grade plumes are not what I need for ostrich heads. Consequently, I buy large ostrich-feather dusters in a local supermarket. These would be listed as second grade by a material supplier, but for my purpose they are ideal. But inflation is coming to the fore, because in the past year the producers have been putting several rows of ostrich around a center bundle of rooster-neck hackle to save on the ostrich feathers. If one is lucky, though, as I was recently, this center will be dark furnace and just right for several steelhead patterns.

Some ostrich plumes are a very deep natural gray and these are used only for wing cases on the Black Drake Nymph. Some are a silvery gray, and these I dye black. Do not boil ostrich; keep the dye bath at simmer heat and rotate the duster till it looks black as midnight. I use nearly twice as much dye in the same amount of water for ostrich as I would for any other material. This is done so the dye will take well without the usual boiling.

I like to dye ostrich on a windy day, the windier the better. Fasten the duster handle to something outside where the wind can whip the plumes dry and they will fluff out naturally. Otherwise, you must shake, beat, and rub the plumes all during the drying process or the flues matt to the quill.

Few fly fishermen in the West have not encountered the big spring hatch of the Dark Stone, generally referred to as

the Dark Salmon Fly. One of the real challenges to the fly tyer when collecting material to imitate this big fellow's wings is finding or dyeing the right shade of dun brown.

In the first edition of *Fuzzy Nymphs,* I referred to the use of coffee-brown Clairol hair dye to get the desired results. This is still quite satisfactory when you are dyeing small pieces of bucktail, but not when you go to large lots or are also dyeing hackle. For this I would rather go to two parts dark brown Rit to one part charcoal gray Rit. You end up with a perfect match for the real fly, and the hackle may also be dyed in the same dye bath.

There are only three colors I have been unable to dye satisfactorily with Rit dye: red, yellow, and orange. For some reason, they always have a dull, lusterless look to them. For the red and orange I now use Herter's acid-vat dye and the same procedure as used on the Rit. The colors are beautiful to behold.

The old gentleman who showed me how to get the most brilliant lemon yellow imaginable into feathers is now fishing across the Great Divide; if he were here he would flay me alive for letting the general public gain this knowledge. Actually, it isn't dye at all, but picric acid, which comes in a bright yellow crystalized powder for use on fresh burns to prevent infection. It has several other uses, but this is one of the more important ones. At the present time, it retails for at least two dollars per ounce and few retail drug stores stock it, not even the big supply houses. Fortunately, I have a friend in the business. He deplores being called a drug salesman, and refers to himself as a pharmaceutical representative. But Bill can always find me an ounce of picric when I need it. One or two words of caution: I had used this stuff for years before I learned that if allowed to get bone dry it will explode on sharp impact, say by dropping the container. I don't know why this is, but now I keep it damp and in the fridge.

Mix one teaspoonful in a quart of hot water. Stir it thoroughly but be careful not to inhale the fumes. I doubt that they will do any real damage, but they tend to choke one up. Don't get any on your skin or clothes or you will be a lemon yellow until it wears off, though it won't burn you or damage clothing.

The nice part about picric acid is that all you have to do is soak the material in it for a few minutes; it needs no boiling. In fact, after I have mixed it in hot water and added the material to be dyed, I go off and forget it for a while. Drain all the unused dye into a glass jar, cap, and store it. You can use it indefinitely by just adding a bit more acid. It may tend to breed a bit of mother eventually, but this can be removed by pouring it through a fine-wire strainer.

Gold Rit dye comes into its own when used for dyeing material for the Golden Stone patterns. While body material for the Golden Stone is now available in all yarn shops, it is still necessary for tyers to dye material for tails, legs, and wing cases for the nymphs, as well as bucktail and hackle for the wet and dry versions. Teal sides, shoulders, gadwall neck, and the darker mallard are all used on the nymphs, and both neck and saddle hackle for the wets and drys.

Among a dozen or so large whitetail deer tails there will always be at least two with pale tan to light brown backs. At this point, you are glad you bought only boned-out tails because you can take a sharp knife and slice the white edges off where they meet the brown. If the tails are not boned, you are in trouble, unless you get busy real fast and use up the

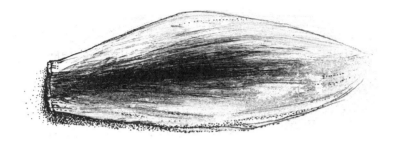

white on Royal Coachman Bucktails or some comparable fly.

With all this aggregate of material for the nymph, wet, and dry versions, you can dye all of it in one operation. I don't mean dump it all in the pot together. Instead, do it this way: Mix a strong dye bath of gold Rit. Dye the bucktail first and get it rather dark. When the desired color is achieved, remove all the bucktail and rinse. Now dye the teal and the hackle last. You are using up some of the dye with each additional material, so each batch comes out a progressively lighter gold. This is the way you want it. Hackle should be the lightest of all.

Blending

I made reference earlier to the discovery that two or three colors of gray or any other set of blended colors were better than an overall cast of one color. I feel this is an important addition to fly-tying lore. The following is a blend of furs I have been using for years and it has turned out to be the most adaptable ever used for the Muskrat and Black Drake nymphs. The fish have also appreciated it. This blend was composed of one-half muskrat belly, one-quarter jackrabbit back sans all guard hairs, and one-quarter western silver-squirrel back, preferably a heavily furred winter skin. The living, breathing appearance of the resulting nymphs would be hard to describe. I don't even want to sell any, but put them aside for my own use.

You have two choices of blending methods. Either hot soap suds in a dishpan, or an electric blender. Both ways have certain advantages. For felting or blending small amounts of fur, the electric blender is tops and all the more so if you want a dry blend for spinning in the old Eastern style on or between a waxed loop. I do not use this method, so if I elect to felt or blend a small amount in the blender, I fill the cup one-third full of hot water, add a tablespoonful of soap flakes, add the fur or whatever else I want to blend, and set the speed on 3. Be sure to hold your hand on the lid because you will have a wild furry milkshake immediately; half a

minute is enough. Pour it through a fine-mesh strainer, run hot water through it, wrap it in paper toweling, squeeze it dry, spread it out for finish drying, and you are ready for tying.

I repeat my caution about using the electric blender: Don't use very much long-haired fur or synthetics or you'll wind up with a rope choking the spinner blades and it is hell to get loose. Still and all, when I want to felt or blend several ounces of material, I much prefer a big dishpan.

The back fur from an early spring groundhog or woodchuck blended with either muskrat or beaver belly makes a fine Fledermouse dubbing. Another is muskrat or beaver, or both blended with brown mink. A local rabbitry gave me a bunch of raw skins once, both black and white. The white can be dyed any color. The black I was doubtful of until I tried bleaching it. By mixing the twenty-volume peroxide with the Basic White powder mentioned previously, I was able to get several colors in the brown-to-tan color spectrum, all based on how long it was treated.

A medium brown was better to blend with muskrat or beaver for the Fledermouse than was natural brown mink. If left in a few more minutes till it became a golden brown, it blended well for the Hare's Ear.

If you live in a city that boasts a poodle parlor and you know one of the operators, you are in luck. Poodle combings not only spin into fine nymphs, but make just as good a binder as jackrabbit when a small amount is mixed with beaver or muskrat belly. Use silver poodle for this; apricot poodle for spinning shrimp. These hairs also dye quite well but require a bit longer boiling. I have a friend who operates a big pet hospital so you know where I get my poodle combings.

Bleaching

Since the publication of the second edition of this book, I have learned a great deal about bleaching techniques. I used to waste a considerable amount of material in my attempts to bleach it, but this is no longer the case. On a lot of materials, the end results are not always what one expects. For example, I started a series of experiments on the premise that if I bleached a gray fur or hair it would end up a lighter shade of gray. So far this has never happened. Every fur or hair—black, gray, or brown—winds up brown, tan, or ginger. In fact, if bleached long enough, dark brown mink will be the same shade of tan that muskrat or beaver belly will be at some stage along the route. Furriers and dyers have the formulas and procedures to bleach beaver and muskrat to an eggshell white, but you might as well try to break into Fort Knox as attempt to learn how they do it. It is far easier to visit

one of the small manufacturing furriers in any large city and offer to buy the scraps you need in the wanted colors. It's amazing what you can come up with for a buck or two: blue mink, chinchilla, all shades of fox, white muskrat, all shades of beaver—the variety is almost endless, and the furrier is generally glad to clear out unusable material.

Probably the one most important thing I have learned is this: in bleaching, do it as fast as possible. This means *everything*. For this reason you must keep a pound of Basic White booster powder on hand. Also, quart-size bottles of twenty-volume hydrogen peroxide. Try to get on the good side of a beauty shop manager (maybe it would be safer to have your wife or girlfriend do it), because you can only buy the Basic White from this source and you can also get the peroxide much cheaper than anywhere else, in the quart size at that. This compound, which looks like watery white gravy, does very well on all hairs, including polar bear: a half hour in Basic White turns it pure white. I don't just soak the material. Rather, I pull on a pair of long rubber household gloves, mix the gravy in a tall three-gallon plastic bucket and proceed to spend a full half hour rubbing, grinding, and squeezing the gravy through every piece in the bucket.

One of the quickest materials for reaction is bucktail. When I want ginger for Light Caddis wings, I bleach the whole tail, the white as well as the brown. The white will come out almost translucent and the brown will reach the ginger color I want in fifteen minutes.

White calf or kip tails treated for forty minutes will not only be clear white, but so translucent as to make a good substitute for polar bear, and do we need that.

A few years ago a local friend made an extensive hunting foray to the Northwest Territories and was lucky enough to bag a Stone sheep. Have you ever wished for a tough, fine, but hollow hair that would be suitable for small dry-fly wings? Well, here it is. The right texture and length comes off the side of the hindquarters, a beautiful blue-gray that is perfect for Blue Duns, Blue Uprights, Blue Quills, Black Gnats, et al., with the plus that it can be bleached in twenty minutes to a pale ginger that is perfect for all flies calling for a ginger-colored wing.

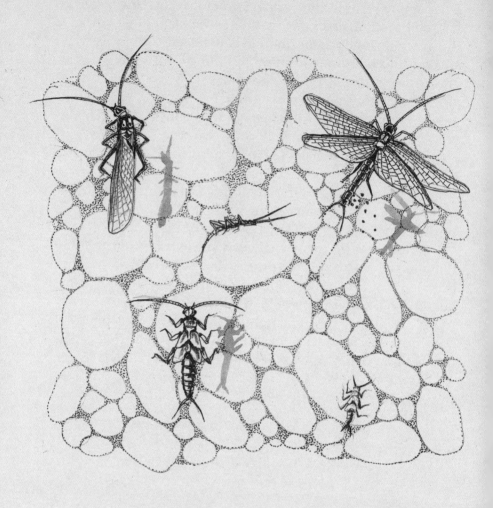

Stoneflies

(Order Plecoptera)

I stressed in the Introduction that intermittently throughout this section there would be many important changes from the text of the first, second, and third editions, and from here on the reader will find largely a new book, reflecting the advances in fly tying that have come at an increasing rate over the last decade. New ideas, new concepts for dressing a hook, plus a host of new materials have been made available since my first experiences. And of course, a lot of the old standby materials, such as Nymo and certain feathers banned from importation, are no longer available. But look around, we will find something to take their places, and it may be even better than the original. One place this is most obvious is in body materials for the original patterns. Many of the dressings I list in succeeding chapters call for commercial knitting yarns where I had formerly used a spinning noodle. You could create the same colors from natural furs, of course, but the objective is the same: to get a fuzzy body effect.

The Dark Stonefly
(Pteronarcys californica)

This is the largest of all western stoneflies, and is eclipsed in size only by the *Pteronarcys dorsata* indigenous to eastern waters. The giant hatches of this big stone on the Madison, Big Hole, and Gunnison are legend.

But let no one think we cannot equal the Yellowstone area rivers with the hatches here in central Oregon. The Williamson, Deschutes, Wood, Upper Rogue, and Umpqua Rivers all have nearly blizzard hatches of Dark Stones. Some years ago above Union Creek on the North Fork of the Rogue an emergence was so heavy that thousands of adults crawling across the highway caused several cars to skid and crash.

The Dark Stone is also known all over the West as the Dark Salmon Fly. This big fellow in the adult stage has a tangerine orange belly and grayish back with four long, flat dun-colored wings. The females may reach two inches in length.

When it comes to describing the nymph coloration, we have a dilemma. The color of the backs in different waters is fairly constant: some shade of dark chocolate brown, often heavily mottled. But the undersides may vary from off white through various shades of cream to orangish mottling on the thorax. This means the tyer and user must simulate local conditions—there can be no set rules.

Of all the feathers used in my nymph tying, shoulder feathers from a Chinese or Mongolian cock pheasant—what we call locally "church windows"—would have to rate the tops. These have pale tan to golden brown mottling in the arch, resembling the art glass in church windows. Generally speaking, they must be dyed dark brown, but the mottling remains clearly visible.

Tying the Dark Stone Nymph

Hook: #2 to #6, the #2 in 3XL; the #4 and #6 in 4XL, and all on 2XS Improved Sproats or comparable hooks.
Tying Thread: Pale cream or maize.
Tails: Four to six flues from a church window, not over one-half inch long. All stoneflies have but two tails, but a few more look "buggier," and as long as the fish don't mind, I won't quibble over a few more.
Ribbing: Medium tan thread, preferably silk buttonhole twist attached at bend of hook.
Body: A new yarn called Dazzle-Aire, available at K-Mart, J. C. Penney, and probably many more stores that sell yarns, is what I use. This synthetic has a sheen almost exactly like seal fur. If it were available in all the colors I need, I would use nothing else for all my tying with one exception: where

tinsel bodies are required.

Tie in a half-inch wide strip from a dark mottled turkey tail feather by the tip end. Now, three-eighths of an inch from the hook eye, tie in a piece of light cream Dazzle-Aire yarn. Use regular four-strand for large hooks; the three-strand baby-yard type lends itself well to #8 and smaller. Apply a heavy coat of cement to the hook and wind the yarn tightly to the rear of the hook or just to where the turkey strip is tied in. Put another coat of cement on the inner body and wind the yarn back to where you started. About one-third of the way back, start expanding the body by overlapping the yarn. The body should be slightly tapered over its full length.

All ribbing is tied in right after the tails, if any, and on the *back* side of the hook, working away from the tyer so the first turn of ribbing starts on the bottom.

Now take a smooth-jawed pair of pliers (chain-nosed type) and flatten the entire body. Pull the turkey back over the top of the body and tie it down. Rib the body with ribbing thread a minimum of nine turns.

Legs: Apply about six flues from the church window on each side as legs, slanted back and a bit downward. They should be one-third the length of the body.

Wing Case: From your original church window you should have enough of the center part of the feather remaining for the wing case, around a half-inch long and covering one-third of the front end of the body. I never tie in wing pads the way most instruction manuals suggest. Instead, I prefer the wing cases to be free to vibrate in the current.

As a general practice, I again flatten the entire body at this point in order to press the ribbing thread deeply into the nymph. Once all that cement sets up it will be practically indestructible. The head should be long and flattened, if possible, before tying off. Apply a coat of clear cement and let it dry. Then apply a heavy coat of dark brown cement to the top and sides. The color should match the brown of the back.

Tying The Dark Stone Adult, Wet Version

Hook: Use same size and type of hooks as used for the nymph.
Tying Thread: Black.
Tails: None; the tails are so short on the adult they can be dispensed with altogether, and I find the fish don't mind.
Ribbing: Use same color of ribbing thread as for the nymph.
Body: Yarn in two colors, tangerine or apricot. Buy it in orlon or nylon, as it is unavailable in Dazzle-Aire. The body

of the adult can be tied identically to the nymph's, except it is not two-tone top and bottom. The female has a lead gray back, but you can get this effect with a perma-color marking pencil.
Legs: Hackle should be very dark furnace and one size narrower than usual. That is, use a size 6 hackle on a #4 hook, and so on.
Wings: Dye a very dark-backed whitetailed deer tail in one part charcoal gray to two parts dark brown and the result should be a deep dun, an exact counterpart of the adult's wings.

Do not overwing the stones—none of them—because looking up at the sky through the wings the veins are about all that are visible. Wings should be not over a half-inch longer than the body, and should be flared at least three-quarters of an inch wide at the rear.
Head: Fill the hair at the head full of heavy cement and, before you make the final run of thread up to the finishing point, flatten it if possible. Tie it off underneath, just in front of the hackle. Lacquer the head heavily and let it dry. The

western Dark Stoneflies all have a bright hot orange spot on top of the head. I paint a band here just in front of the wing—not all the way around, just across the top and down the sides. Liking fluorescence, here I use a brilliant watercolor, which dries immediately and the head is then given another coat of clear lacquer all over. It will not dissolve the watercolor band, and you can see that orange cap in water of average clarity fifty feet away.

Contrary to the old eastern and European methods of fishing both nymphs and wet flies upstream, sometimes tumbling them along the bottom, both the nymph and adult Dark Stone are seldom fished more than a foot deep.

Cast straight across the current and allow the fly or nymph to swing in the current, always on a tight line and using an eight-pound tippet. The strikes most often occur at the forty-five-degree angle, or when the fly or nymph has reached its greatest depth and starts to rise. These strikes can be explosive, and often have shattering results, both to your tackle and your mental equilibrium.

A weight-forward wet-tip line is almost a must, and if you are fishing especially heavy water, a Hi-D tip.

I do not tie a dry version of the Dark Stone. The big wet will produce just as well and also provoke larger fish than any dry version. Plus, such a big dry is too hard to float.

The Golden Stonefly
(Calineuria californica)
(Doroneuria baumanni)

As stated in the Introduction, there will be some changes made, and a lot of them occur in discussing the Golden Stone.

During the actual time of going to press on the third edition, a whole new classification took place on all western stoneflies, too late to include it in the book. All to the good; I would be able to add the following to the fourth edition.

A good friend of mine, one Al Kyte of Moraga, California, a baseball coach and also an instructor at the University of California at Berkeley, sent me a completely new list of the new classifications of all western stoneflies. No more *Acroneuria* west of Colorado. Further, our Golden Stone had been split into two genera, the *Calineuria californica* and the *Doroneuria baumanni.*

This cleared up a past problem for me. Why did our local Goldens emerge in early June on the big river, while on one main tributary and Wood River they emerge six weeks later? Research proved this to be the same genus, only governed by a large difference in water temperature. The big river, the Williamson, is ten degrees warmer than Spring Creek or Wood River, but all emergences are over by August fifteenth.

The dates are pretty much constant east of the Cascades; not so on the west slope, where the hatch on the Rogue and North Umpqua starts in September and lasts till mid-October—but this one turns out to be *Doroneuria baumanni.*

According to Al Kyte it takes a microscope and an entomologist to tell the differences, and I agree. I have never seen the nymph of the *Doroneuria,* so I can't say there is any real difference to the *Calineuria,* but there is some difference in the color of the underside of the abdomen on the two genera. The *Doroneuria* is more of a deep amber yellow, and the *Calineuria* is a real antique gold. Also, their habits of emergence are identical.

I ask you, have you ever seen a Golden Stone shuck or nymph husk on a rock or high up on a willow like the *Pteronarcys*? No. And you never will because this stonefly in both genera leaves the case on the stream's bottom, shoots to the surface, and emerges on the wing. The first time I witnessed this astounding performance I thought there must be a mistake. Doesn't everyone know that all stonefly nymphs have to climb out of the water to hatch? Well, it just ain't so.

The first time I saw this emergence was on the Maple Pool right behind the number one cabin at Steamboat Inn on the Umpqua. The steelhead were not hitting, so I was fishing a "Dry" for the ten-inch or so natives. The pool was fairly smooth, so when a Golden Stone suddenly flew right out of the water, I thought at first I had imagined it. "Maybe he got swept under up at the falls at the Mott," I thought. But then a second and a third followed the first, which made me realize I was seeing history made. Later, I checked this out with two local riverboat guides. Had they seen this type of emergence? "Hell, yes. All the time in June," they said.

Later yet, I had a helluva time convincing Ernie Schweibert of this, but when I presented so much corroborative testimony, he finally admitted, "Well, we never know it all."

The finished Golden Stone Nymph, as seen from above.

Tying the Golden Stone Nymph

Hook: Tie the Golden Stone on #4 or #6, 3XL–2XS Improved Sproat; Wright and McGill's #1206 is the ideal hook here. Buz's Fly Shop, 805 West Tulare Avenue, Visalia, California 93277, is one of the few shops that carry this hook.

Thread: Antique gold silk size A, #3715 by Belding.
Ribbing: Thread of same color and number, buttonhole twist.

Use barred teal dyed a rich gold with Rit dye for the tail, back, legs, and wing cases.

Since the first edition of this book was published, many and various types of yarns have appeared on the market that are suitable for the Golden Stone. The one I am currently using is a very brilliant gold orlon, almost luminous. But no matter what yarn you use, buy it as fuzzy as possible; after all, this book is all about fuzzy nymphs.

In sorting teal for the big side feathers for backs and the shorter well-barred type for tails and legs, you generally find some short neck feathers much darker than the larger ones.

The Golden Stone Nymph before applying the back feather.

These are ideal for the Golden Stone wing cases. Use the whole feather, and make the wing cases one-third the length of the body. Do not trim the ends.

The dressing of this nymph is identical to the Dark Stone. Only the colors and size of the hook are different.

Fishing technique for the Golden Stone Nymph is also identical to the Dark Stone. It just emerges a month later, generally from June fifth till the fourth of July, varying, of course, with latitude and elevation.

Tying the Adult Golden Stone, Wet Version

The Golden Stone wet fly is a most versatile pattern. It's all antique gold in coloration, not too far off from the more

The wet version of the Adult Golden Stone

The Golden Stone Wet with the body yarn tied in. Note the position of the ribbing.

yellowish grasshoppers that arrive some six weeks later; but also when you need a big Light or Cinnamon Caddis and find your fly book vacant of the pattern, the Golden Stone can serve as an acceptable substitute.

Hook: Should be the same as used for the nymph. No tail is needed, the same as for the wet Dark Stone.

Body: The body material, ribbing thread, and working thread are identical to the nymph. No two-tone body is needed, but fill it full of cement and flatten it as you do the

The Golden Stone Wet body properly flattened. This is also the shape of the flattened-nymph bodies.

nymph. Dye a soft webby neck hackle one shade darker gold than the body and use it one size smaller than the hook. The hackle on the big long-bodied stones should cover not more than half of the body when activated in the water.

Wing: Gold-dyed hair from the back of a light brown deer tail. If this hair is too dark to dye into gold, bleach it with twenty-volume hydrogen peroxide and a teacupful of Basic White powder. Use one quart of the peroxide to the cup of powder. With long rubber household gloves, constantly

Hackle applied to the Golden Stone Wet.

work the gravy-like mixture through the bucktail. A few minutes in this solution will lighten the hair enough to dye it the dark gold color required.

As a general rule, I bleach a dozen tails, which requires a half-gallon of peroxide and a full measuring cup of Basic White. Half are removed when light enough for the Golden Stone, the other half are left in the bleach till they are light enough for Light Caddis wings, which I tie by the gross. This way, you kill two birds with one stone, as all the action of the

Bucktail wing on the finished Golden Stone Wet.

bleach takes place in twenty minutes and is then discarded.

Wings are the same length in proportion to the body as the Dark Stone, also flared.

Head: The head is flattened, which helps to flare the wing, and it gets three coats of the heavy head cement. The silk thread used in tying this fly soaks up the first coat, unlike nylon, so that it looks like there's no cement on it, hence the third coat to give it gloss.

Tying the Adult Golden Stone, Dry Version

This is one of the great ones all along the Pacific Coast states, and like the wet version, can also be pressed into use as a substitute for the Yellow Grasshopper and the Light or Cinnamon Caddis.

Hook: #8 and #10, 3XL regular weight wire #38941 Mustad Sproat. To my knowledge, no hook is made in fine wire of this length or I would be using it, if only for greater floatability.

Tail: There is little deviation in body colors from the wet version, but here we add a tail just to help support the float. Tail of very stiff dry-fly quality hackle not over one-quarter inch in length, and thick for better support on the water.

Body: Antique gold color yarn is available in three-strand baby yarn and it is ideal for the body on this dry fly. The one I am currently using is Berella by Bernat in one-ounce skeins. On the label it says, "Fingering Yarn 60% orlon, 40% nylon, Color, Old Gold. Ideal for babies." It is also ideal for Golden Stone drys, or wets, for that matter.

Legs: This fly requires two gold-dyed hackles: one for palmer ribbing of the body, and one for a front collar forward of the wing. After tying in the tail, start body one-quarter inch back from eye of hook; wind to the tail and back one turn. Don't forget the cement between the two layers of the body. With the body yarn, tie in the butt of a long web-free gold saddle and have the overwound hackle quill long or you will have it pull out when you wind it. Reason: when you have wound the body yarn back to where it started and have tied it off, you must flatten the body before you palmer the hackle. See? That long-butted quill nearly as long as the body just gave you insurance that it won't pull out.

Palmer the body, tie off, and half-hitch your working thread. Now, with your scissors shear off all hackle on top and a wee bit down the sides. Grasp the fly between your thumb and forefinger. Squeeze all remaining hackle together and shear it off right at the bottom of the hook because an even clip helps to make the fly ride upright.

You will note this version of the Golden Stone has no rib. The center quill of the palmer acts as the rib.

Wing: Dry is the same as wet; use the second hackle, which should be of super-dry-fly quality to wind as a collar in front of the wing. This hackle should be a ten, or a #8 fly; a twelve for a #10.

It is not necessary to flatten the heads on this one, though when I get a custom order from some persnickety customer, I give myself a bit more room for a long head, as on the wet, and flatten it. I very much doubt if this added touch makes any difference to the fish.

This dry is about the only fly I fish from mid-June to mid-July.

The Little Yellow Stonefly
(Isoperla marmona)

The Little Yellow Stonefly seems to have almost worldwide distribution. It is a common fly in the British Isles and is discussed and pictured in Alfred Ronald's book *Flyfisher's Entomology,* published early in the nineteenth century. This would lead to the conclusion that it occurs around the globe at approximately the same latitudes. In such a large family there are no doubt many genera, but the one under discussion is the most important here in the West. The trout love them, both the nymphs and all versions of the adult.

Tying the Little Yellow Stone Nymph

Hook: #10 or #12, 3XL regular weight wire as a rule, but if you fish fast water, a 2XS hook may have its advantages.

Tying Thread: Amber yellow nylon; there is no chartreuse nylon but the amber yellow seems to absorb some color from

the chartreuse yarn body so that they harmonize.

Ribbing: The working thread is also used for the segmented ribbing, which should be very close—at least eight turns. This means that 3X Monocord is the ideal working thread because its small diameter will not hide the chartreuse yarn body too much.

Tail, Back, Legs, and Wing Cases: Dyed barred mallard. It took a bit of experimenting to arrive at the right color, which is best described as a dirty chartreuse: a blend of two parts chartreuse Rit to one of tan is the right answer.

A mottled back of the dyed mallard is applied in the same manner as on the Dark Stone and Golden Stone, and is segmented with the working thread. Bodies are always flattened on all stones in any stage, nymph or adult. When choosing a feather for the legs, pick one with flue long enough so the butts may be bent back, tied down, and clipped off one-third the length of the body. You will never pull out or lose legs applied in this manner. This idea is feasible on but a few patterns and in the smaller sizes, as few feathers have flues long enough.

Synthetic two-ply or three-ply yarns are available in chartreuse, a pale greenish yellow, in almost any big yarn mart. The same color and type of yarn is also used on the wet and dry versions of the adult.

Heads: The head should be a bit oversized and well flattened.

This is an emergent nymph with fully developed wing cases and is fished in the top film in early evening. After sundown the adult versions seem to be preferred.

Tying the Little Yellow Stonefly, Wet Version (Female)

Hook: #12, 3XL, #38941 by Mustad.
Tying Thread: Same as for the nymph.
Tail: In order to give the effect of the coloration of the female, it is necessary to simulate the egg sac, and this is done by tying in a very small bunch of crimson hackle as the first step. Clip it off blunt so that it is one-sixteenth inch long. Over this, tie in a tail of wet-fly-quality hackle fibers three times as long as the clipped crimson. Color should be honey dun.
Ribbing: Same as the tying thread.
Body: Same as for the nymph. Carry the tying thread forward to where the body will end and tie in the body yarn. Keep all stonefly bodies almost the same diameter over their full length, allowing for a small taper at the rear end.
Wing: One wing only is needed: this is so it will be more nearly transparent. Use the tip of a pale cree neck hackle for this and lay it flat on top of the body, reaching just to the tip of the tail.

Legs: Most wet flies have the hackle applied before the wing, but on this pattern you can't make the wing lie flat on the body if the hackle is applied first. Wind a soft size-ten pale cree hackle in front of the wing and overwind it with the working thread to make it lie back á la wet-fly style. Again, the head should be a bit oversized and flattened.

Tying the Little Yellow Stone, Dry Version Fore and Aft (Female)

One big advantage of using this pattern is its long appearance, covering almost two months of the fishing season. Its first appearance is generally around June fifth and a few will still be around early in August. Many places in the West it is known as the willowfly, due to its habit of swarming among the streamside willows. It is recognized, however, that there are several other and larger stones that are locally known as willowflies nationwide.

Hook: 10XL and 1XF, #60 by Wright & McGill. This is a semi-forged Improved Sproat, the only one of its kind and it lends itself well to the tying of medium-sized dry flies #8 to #14.

Tying Thread: Same as for the nymph; ribbing is also the same.

Body: Same as for the nymph; the egg sac and tail are applied the same as on the wet. Now wind on a size twelve very stiff-flued dry-quality pale cree neck hackle. Try to get five turns well bunched. Tie off and tie in a three-inch piece of your working thread for ribbing. Carry the thread to where the front of the body will be and tie in the body yarn. Now create a body identical with the previously described wet and apply ribbing.

Wings: Last, wind a size ten neck hackle in front of the body. A note here: All of my dry patterns have the hackles applied concave side forward so the flue will point forward as the legs of the natural insect do. I know that according to tradition this is heresy, but I have always been a rebel, and of late years I find I have a lot of company.

Head: The head on the dry can be a bit smaller than on the nymph and wet versions but should still be flattened.

Little Brown or Red Stonefly Nymph
(Taeniopteryx pacifica)

This is the only stonefly nymph presented here that does not have a two-toned body. True, there is a slight difference in the overall shade between the back and belly colors, but not enough to create the need for different colors in the imitation.

There is some argument, which I am inclined to think is valid, that both the nymph and adult may vary considerably in color from reddish brown to a dark seal brown with almost no reddish tinge at all. All I have collected in central Oregon and northern California have been of the dark seal in color.

This little stone, also like the Little Yellow Stonefly, has a long emergence season. It has one advantage over the Little Yellow Stone in that it is a midday hatch, seeming more like the Dark Stone and Golden Stone to prefer bright sunlight in order to make its debut into the adult stage. Seasonal emergence dates start early in May and may appear intermittently till September.

Tying the Little Brown Stonefly Nymph

Hook: Tie the nymph on a 3XL, #12 Improved Sproat #38941 by Mustad.

Tying Thread: Seal brown nylon. With so many tying

threads coming and going on and off the market it becomes necessary to choose from what is available in the color needed. Formerly, when Belding's Nymo was available to all, it was no problem to say such and such a color and number and there were no problems. But not today. So I will list the name, color, type of yarn, and manufacturer of the yarn used for bodies of the Little Brown Stone Nymph, and also for the adult dry. This yarn is two-ply, very fuzzy, 67% Mohair, 33% Orlon Acrylic, and comes in many colors. Trade name: Frostlon Petite Spinnerin by Spinnerin Yarn Co., Inc., Hackensack, New Jersey, 07606.

Body: Seal brown yarn.

Tails, Legs, and Wing Cases: Tippets from the brown neck ruff on the Chinese cock pheasant. These feathers may be a bit pale, so dye them in Rit dark brown. The top of the feather has a purple iridescence, which will remain after dying, and on the wing cases this tends to create a more attractive nymph. Tails are three-sixteenths of an inch long. Rib the body with working thread, and closely, at least seven or eight turns. Flatten it, as in all stones. The body is slender with little taper, but with a somewhat oversized head and flared wing cases; observing it from a top view it appears more portly than it really is.

The flues on the pheasant feathers are too short for the procedure used on the Little Yellow Stone, so the legs and

wing cases must be tied in separately. The legs should be half the length of the body. The wing cases should cover half of the body and be a bit flared.

This fly is an emergent pattern, to be fished dead drift just under the top film between 11:00 A.M. and 2:00 P.M. daylight saving time, and produces best in bright sunlight.

These little stones are prevalent in fairly fast riffles, so I do not think they need any agitation by the angler. Being so small an insect, with plenty of water movement it would seem superfluous for the angler to add any unnatural action.

Tying the Little Brown Stone or Little Red Stone, Dry Version

There will be no wet version of this stonefly offered. The nymph and corresponding dry are so consistently effective during their seasons that it would be somewhat like carrying coals to Newcastle to put a wet version in conflict with the nymph, especially since both would be fished in a like manner.

The hook size is #14, 3XL, #38941 Improved Sproat by Mustad. The working thread, tails, and rib are identical for the nymph. In fact, when the body is done, the tyer can make up his mind, "Is this one to be a nymph or a dry?"

If you have the shekels to be able to afford a super-grizzly saddle patch, here is where you gain added bounty on your investment. Those little short dark spades up front are perfect for the single flat wing tied down flat on the body just the same as you did the cree on the Little Yellow Stone. Wings on the Little Brown Stone are a dark mottled gray, and dark-phase grizzly matches them perfectly.

Wind a size twelve or fourteen dark grizzly saddle hackle in front of the wing as a collar, using at least five turns. Wind on a fairly large head and flatten it. Lacquer, and you are ready to go fishing.

Caddisflies

(Order Trichoptera)

It has long been my considered opinion that this order of aquatic insects has never been accorded its proper place in the food chain not only of the various trouts, but of many other of the game fishes. Bass, bluegills, and perch all feed on caddis in warmer waters, such as Oregon's lowland lakes and streams, the year round.

When I speak of caddis in northern California, Oregon, and Washington, and even far up into British Columbia, I am not referring to any of the microcaddis. The caddis I refer to are the larger families found almost exclusively on the West Coast. My treatment of the caddis family will, in fact, cover only two families and a total of three or four genera.

At least three of these genera are as yet unclassified. The first of these is a member of the Rhyacophilidae family and is the giant *Rhyacophila grandis,* which may vary in length from twenty-five to thirty-five millimeters from the front of the head to the rear end of the wings. Bodies are a full quarter-inch in diameter. The wings are highly mottled in shades of brown, almost exactly like a dark turkey tail. Legs and antennae are mottled likewise. The bodies are a medium gray-green with the accent on the green.

Insofar as I can learn, this big fellow is found only in the West Coast states and British Columbia, and, as usual, in Canada it receives the British treatment and is called the Green Sedge.

The Green Rockworm Larva
(Family, Rhyacophilidae; Genus, varied)

This caddis is tied only in the larval form and the adult. The Rhyacophilidae family are the only caddis that do not construct a case. Rather, they are free foragers on the bottom of any stream they inhabit, and as such, vulnerable to the trout all the year through. This also accounts for the Green Rockworm Larva's fish-taking effectiveness, in as many as three sizes, to wit: #8, #10, and #12. The larvae are native to nearly all freestone riffles, preferably two to four feet in depth.

This is the only pattern out of my twenty-five originals that is fished in the original upstream fashion recommended by G. E. M. Skues and Ed Hewitt, and here I go all out on their methods because the trout get very little chance to ever capture this caddis in the pupal form. But it is vulnerable as it crawls on the bottom from one protective rock to the next, and especially during bright sunny days between eleven and two daylight saving time. I fish a #8 on a seven and one-half foot leader with a 4X tippet and a Hi-D Wet-tip line.

Casting on a slight diagonal to my right and upstream (I'm lefthanded) and never using more than fifteen feet of line, I let the larva roll along the bottom, back to me. It is given no action whatever, just allowed to roll with the current, and I watch for only one thing: a silvery flash where I know my nymph is in the current.

This flash tells me a trout has rolled slightly to engulf my offering, and I strike. This method is far more productive than watching for a movement of your line where it enters the water.

At pupation time the larva walls itself into a small crack between stones or stationary debris and creates an almost transparent cocoon for itself. You can see the bright insect green of the pupa right through the thin walls. This transformation usually takes place close to the water's surface, so then the pupa has only a short dash to the surface and in the matter of a few seconds is on the wing.

Tying the Green Rockworm

Hook: #8, #10, or #12 #1206 Sproat, 2XS and 3XL. You would fish the #12 in April, the #10 in May and June, and the #8 in July during emergences.
Tying Thread: Black.
Ribbing: Blue-green thread, darker than the body.

Body: Green Spray Mohlon, a true insect green when it's wet. If this yarn is not available, substitute a comparable shaggy yarn. The finished product must be very rough. Segment the body with nine turns of the ribbing thread; I do not construct a thorax because I find it unnecessary. The body should taper slightly at both ends.

Legs: Turn the hook upside down in the vise and tie in a half dozen or more legs of bluish green dyed barred teal.

Head: Finish off the head as for the Muskrat described earlier: about four black ostrich flues twisted and wound in front of the body and legs, about three turns. Tie it off, lacquer the head, and it is ready to catch a trout.

Tying the Green Caddis Adult, Wet Pattern

Hook: Size #6, regular length; as to its weight, let the speed and depth of the water be your guide. It should be submerged anywhere from three inches to one foot deep when fished.

Tying Thread: Black.

Tails: No tails on any caddis at any time.

Body: Any fuzzy yarn a medium grayish green in color. Start body in front where it will end, wind into a coat of heavy cement to the curve of the hook, make one turn back and tie in tip of a size eight dark furnace saddle hackle. Wind the body back to the front, tie it off and palmer the saddle hackle all the way to the front of the body. Your hackle should be long enough to make five turns with enough left over to make three more turns in front of the body. If your palmer hackle is not long enough, add a short furnace in front and tie in the butt dry-style to wind it. It's much easier.

Wings: I lay aside special eastern brown-backed deer tails for this particular fly. These tails must be quite dark, with what I would term bronze tips, but deep gray at the base. The idea is to simulate the mottling of a bronze turkey tail feather in two-tone browns. This is exactly the color of the big *Rhyacophila grandis* wings.

Tying the Green Caddis Adult, Dry Pattern

Hook: #8, 1XF and 1XL #60 Sproat by Wright & McGill.
Tying Thread: Black.
Body: Yarn of same color as the wet, but if possible a pure acrylic for better floating qualities. The body techniques are basically the same as for the wet fly, but the dark furnace palmer hackle here must only be wide enough to reach the point of the hook and of stiff dry-fly quality—no web whatever. Palmer hackle on the dry is tied in butt first. Leave a bit extra room for the wing and head because another stiff hackle is wound in front of the wing and this one should be just slightly wider than the palmered one. The purpose of this extra hackle is to give the floating fly a bit more elevation in front, like the living insect.

Dark Caddis Emergent
(Family, Limnephilidae; Genus, Dicosmoecus)

This giant of the caddis family makes its first appearance during the legal fishing season, about August first. Actually, there is a March emergence of this species on Oregon streams, but it is of no importance to the angler unless one considers that it comes at a time when not much else is available in food and so tends to produce fat trout by the time the season opens in late April. So far as my untrained eye can tell, they are identical except for the color of their heads: the March occurrence has a burnt orange head, the August one has a black head. But what is important to the angler is that once it appears, it continues to do so until the season ends, in most western states October thirty-first.

This caddis is one of the two real monsters of the order. From the front of the head to the rear of the wing tips, they often are a full inch in length. However, I do not tie the emergent larger than a #6, though a #4 would not be too large for a good simulation.

Tying the Dark Caddis Emergent

Hook: #6 or #8. The #8 should be on a #3906B Mustad Sproat; the #6 on a #3906 Mustad Sproat. If the #8 is 1XL, the finished emergent will end up the same length on both hooks.

Tying Thread: Black.

Body: Yarn a pale burnt orange, ribbed with orange Monocord of the same color. Not much contrast is wanted, the main thing desired is the segmented effect of all insects. Shape and taper of body is identical with the Green Caddis discussed earlier.

Legs and Wings: In front of the body wind four turns of spey furnace, and it should have a flue wide enough to completely mask all of the body and even a bit to the rear of the hook. Here is where you get rid of a bunch of junk hackle after you have used up all the good web-free furnace saddle.

For emergent caddis patterns, the more web the better. With the hackle in place, twist it all toward you till each flue sticks straight out at right angles to the hook. This little procedure eliminates the swirling effect when you look at it from the front.

Now remove the hook from the vise and clip off all the flues on both top and bottom. In other words, leave just a thick bunch on each side to simulate the already emerged legs and wings.

Head: Last, spin about four black ostrich flues in front of the hackle and try to cover up the ends of the trimmed hackle. Tie it off and the emergent is finished.

This bug is fished with a floating line, and all of the leader should float except an eighteen-inch tippet of Quik-

Starting a #6 Dark Caddis: The body yarn is tied in and ready for winding.

Sink Berkley Trilene. Your leader need not be over nine feet and about 3 or 4X at the tippet.

If there is an emergence, almost invariably you will see trout swirling just subsurface, so drop your offering three feet upstream from a swirl, allow it to sink a foot, then retrieve it fast in two-inch jerks. I find the best approach is to cast upstream with a very short line, rarely over twenty feet. This method is especially deadly on those old, smart browns.

Tying the Dark Caddis Adult, Wet Version

Hook: Sizes can be varied, and either regular wet-fly weight or 2XS, #4 to #8 inclusive. The #8 is stretching the range

Dark Caddis body finished with dark furnace saddle hackle tied in by tip under the second turn of body yarn.

The Dark Caddis Wet with palmered hackle wound and tied off.

somewhat, although most of my dry versions are tied thus. But this is only to obtain better floating qualities.

Body: Burnt orange yarn; if obtainable in the right color, use a fuzzy mohair because it will saturate better than the acrylics.

Except for the body color, all tying procedure is identical with the Green Caddis: dark furnace hackle and bucktail wing, though it would be better to use the darkest bucktail

The #6 Dark Caddis Wet with dark-bronze-tipped bucktail wing.

available. I tie one version of this fly I call the Fall Caddis on a #4 hook with an all sooty black wing. It is highly effective, but I cannot prove it is a bit more productive than the mottled-brown-winged version.

All fishing presentation is identical with the Green Caddis except the fishing hours. Whereas the Green Caddis is best during the sunlight hours, the Dark Caddis only comes into its own after sunset and on until dark.

Tying the Dark Caddis Adult, Dry Version

The best simulation of this dry is tied on a #8 3XL Mustad Sproat #38941.

Tying Thread: Black.

Body: The color is identical with the wet version but here it should be nylon, orlon, or one of the acrylics; just try to get the best floatant qualities. Otherwise, follow the same procedure as used on the Green Caddis: the same narrow furnace hackle and dark bucktail wing with another super-dry hackle collar in front of the wing.

Too many of you readers are top dry-fly experts for me to presume to tell you how to present this fly. Just get to it.

The Light Caddis
(Family, Limnephilidae; Genus, varied)

Why doesn't some accredited aquatic entomologist make a point of spending a few years here on the West Coast and make it his project to study and classify the hundreds of aquatic insects that seem to be strictly indigenous to the Far West? Such a treatise is badly needed, if only to help tyros like myself when I write a book. Here in Oregon we have at least four different genera of the caddis family Limnephilidae that are totally unclassified. In mid-April a giant of this species makes its appearance. This early bird is as large as the big dark caddis and just as clumsy a flyer. One wonders how all of them keep from colliding with one another.

As the spring and summer seasons come and pass, so do

the various species of light caddis. Also, as the season advances, the size of the emergent insects becomes smaller. Colors vary less, but one tied the color of the April hatch and reduced to #8 would be a poor bet for success in October. So before going into tying procedures on this family, it would be best to line them up both to size and color combinations.

The giant April and May hatch is a #4 with a mauve abdomen (pinkish tan), a medium ginger thorax, and a medium ginger wing, with the head as close to wing color as possible.

The June and July hatch is a #6 and all parts are medium ginger. August, September, and October are a #8 and there are apparently two different genera here. Two-thirds of them have an abdomen of tan with a faint greenish tinge in the segments. The balance of the fly is the same medium ginger as the earlier hatches. Then there is a counterpart insofar as legs and wings, but the body on this last one is medium brown with lateral stripes of a faint orange tinge.

The only identification I can give you on this one is Ernie Schwiebert's statement when I showed him specimens in October of 1976: "It is a Limnephilidae." See what I mean?

Tying the Light Caddis Emergent

Hook: Sizes may be #6 down to #8 regular-length shank. In no case should they be tied on too heavy a hook because all are to be fished in the top foot of water.
Tying Thread: Black.
Ribbing: Medium yellow.

Body: Creamy yellow Dazzle-Aire, hackle soft mottled ginger, head black ostrich. Here is where the Dazzle-Aire comes into its own. It is available in a pale creamy yellow color, as nearly identical with the natural as it is possible to get.

Except for more variation in size, a different body color and rib, and the spey hackle collar, this emergent is assembled point by point identically to the Dark Caddis Emergent. The top and bottom on ginger hackle are trimmed the same as the dark version. The silky sheen overlay of the Dazzle-Aire when submerged will give the same effect as the air bubble surrounding the emergent on its fast trip to the surface. I don't know if the trout really appreciate this added touch, but it sure looks good.

While the emergent is fished in the same manner as its darker counterpart, it has a much wider range of presentation, not only in size, but also in effective hours. The various genera of the light caddis seem to have no regular hours of emergence. Morning, high noon, or evening, if the trout are feeding, this emergent will produce. You have only to vary the size to fit the prevailing species.

Tying the Light Caddis Adult, Wet Pattern

As I stated earlier, there is a great disparity of size in the various genera of this family, so it is really almost like telling you how to tie four different flies.

I only attempt to simulate the April and May version in the wet, inasmuch as it is too large to be a good floater no matter what material is used: Size #4, 1XL and 2SX, #1197 Mustad Sproat.

If you can't find any mauve yarn for the abdomen, why not tie it all ginger? I have, and the fish didn't seem to mind. Otherwise, follow the same assembly instructions as for the Dark Caddis. Tying thread should be a light tan and the wing and palmer hackle of medium ginger.

For the June and July version, tie it all medium ginger but on a #6 hook, also a #1197 Sproat. The August, September, and October versions have two overlapping genera as stated earlier, but both of the same size, a #8, #3906B Sproat by Mustad.

What seems to be the more important one is the genus with a greenish tan abdomen and medium ginger thorax, legs, and wings. Browse around the yarn marts and look for a mohair acrylic blend two-ply yarn in tan and pale green combo. I found a few balls of this several years ago and it was perfect for the greenish abdomen version.

The other genus, comparable both in size and color of legs and wings, has a totally different color body, also, it is more streamlined. Body color is a medium brown with faint orange lateral stripes, and I must say getting this effect had me somewhat bugged for a time, but I finally did it. Tie the body of the pale orange color you want on the sides, then, with a medium brown permanent marking pencil, color up the top and bottom and a bit down the sides, also up from the bottom. The lateral stripe should be only one-half as wide as the whole side of the body.

Unfortunately, I have so far been unable to differentiate between the larva, pupa, and emergent of this genus and those of the one with the greenish tan abdomen. So, as long as the trout don't seem to know the difference, why bother?

Tying the Light Caddis Adult, Dry Version

This is often one of the real hot drys all over the West, as its constant emergence from June till November and season's end allows it to fill in when no other hatches of importance are in evidence.

After reading, or maybe skipping, through dozens of volumes on fly tying, entomology, and what have you, I have become convinced that all writers are missing a big bet by not paying more attention to the Trichoptera order. Recently,

Eric Leiser and Larry Solomon came out with their fine volume, *The Caddis and the Angler,* but when I reached the Far West section, there was no mention of any of our big western caddis, with the exception of the Limnephilidae, genus *Dicosmoecus,* and this would not have made the book without the help of Dave McNeese of Salem, Oregon. Unfortunately, Dave was not familiar with the big *Rhyacophila grandis* and the three species of the Limnephilidae we have just been discussing. So, while I cannot classify these last three specifically, perhaps this discussion will help.

We only switch hooks for all dry versions of the June to November Light Caddis. Also add the dry-type hackle collar in front of the wing.

For the June and July #6 or #8 version, use a Wright & McGill #60, 1XF–1XL hook and tie it all medium ginger from start to finish.

As mentioned earlier, the #8 August versions only differ in the body colors. The one departure in hackle color comes on the palmer rib of the caddis with the medium brown body. Color should be as dull a light brown and as narrow as possible so as not to mask the body colors. The front collar should be medium ginger, the same as on the other versions.

With the exception of the King's River Caddis and my two wet versions of the Light and Dark Caddis shown in *The Caddis and the Angler,* no other caddis patterns have palmered bodies. To me, no caddis has top value in its action in or on the water if it is not palmered both wet and dry. I am aware, of course, that ninety percent of all caddis used are tied on hook sizes 12 to 22, but still, all caddis have both slightly fuzzy bodies and scaly wings, plus the fact that the dry versions float much better when palmered.

We have several versions of various microcaddis all up and down the West Coast states, and in areas where there are no versions of the big boys these leetle fellers can be very important in a trout's food cycle. But if the same flies are tied in #4 to #8, the microcaddis go begging for attention. After all, our Oregon trout do not grow to twenty pounds on sirloin tips when plenty of porterhouse is available.

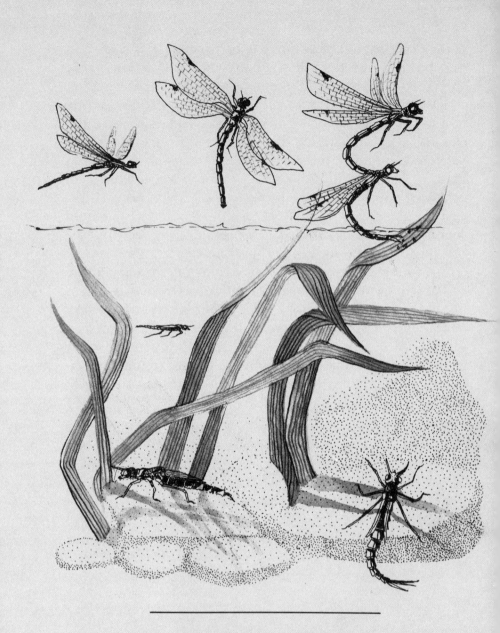

Damselflies
(Order Odonata, Suborder Zygoptera)

The nymphs of the damsel order are far more important in the food chain than most of us realize. On slow-moving streams and reed-bordered lakes and ponds the population of damsel nymphs is almost unbelievable. At the height of their emergence, during the month of June, I have seen them crawl out on the pumice beaches at Oregon's Davis Lake in such number that it reminded me of the boys emerging on the beaches of Normandy.

Only one species of the Zygoptera will be presented here, the *Calopteryx yakima*. This is the one that becomes metallic blue as an adult. On emergence this damsel is a pale grayish green and is very delicate, so much so that I have never seen one on the wing. Rather, they cling to a reed, cattail, or whatever is handy on emergence until exposure to the air turns them blue.

There is a lot of misunderstanding on this point, and I was one of those holding to some erroneous ideas about what took place between the nymph and the blue adult. A newspaper column published daily and syndicated nationwide convinced me that the damsels have a dun stage, the same as mayflies, but a check with Ernest Schwiebert in the fall of 1976 ruled out this possibility. "No way," said Ernie. "Only the mayflies have what we term the dun stage."

Tying the Green Damsel Nymph

Hook: #6 or #8, 3XL, regular-weight wire Improved Sproat #38941 by Mustad.

Tying Thread: #9125 Limerick Green silk by Belding. None of the synthetic threads are made anywhere close to the proper color.

Tail: A short piece of maribou a light golden olive in color, somewhat lighter than the body but never darker. Should be from three-eighths to a half-inch long. I find this kind of tail gives the maximum action desired on this nymph.

Ribbing: Same as tying thread and you simply leave a long butt on it to use later as the rib.

Body: Any of the various acrylics, a medium golden olive cast, and the fuzzier the better. Some years ago I acquired two skeins of this color, which had the name tag "Spicy Lime," and it has been a nemesis to the trout ever since. The body is round, but the rear two-thirds is kept very slender; the front third is built up into a fat thorax just as the natural.
Legs: A medium olive hackle, two shades darker than the tail (barred teal gives the best effect), and just long enough to reach the point of the hook when folded back.
Wing Cases: Maribou fluff two shades darker than the body. The entire color composite ends up with four different colors of golden olive. Wing cases should be one-half the length of the body.

When this nymph is fished with one-inch, very fast jerks of the rod tip and line, it really comes alive and is a top producer over a long season. The first damsels appear early in June and successive hatches occur till October.

I have observed a major emergence of damsels on Oregon's Davis Lake where the reeds were nearly covered with emergents. Then suddenly a whopping big rainbow would charge through the reeds, dumping dozens of the pale greenish damsels in the water, then come tearing back to scoop up a big mouthful for lunch. You may think I am pulling your collective legs on this story, but it is definitely true. Trout are "smart people."

Tying the Green Damsel, Wet Version

The final stage of the damsel, the blue adult, is of little importance in the trout's food chain, being primarily taken when completely spent with their wings outspread on the water. The emergent, however, can be and is highly important in the food chain, especially around reedy shores where the nymph can ascend straight up out of the water and cling to a reed till it becomes a blue adult—which is, incidentally, a very efficient mosquito- and midge-control agent.
Hook: #6 or #8, 3XL, regular Sproat, #38941 by Mustad.

Body: A pale grayish green ribbed with matching tying thread. I can't give you the name or number of it because the spools are not numbered, but Monocord makes one color in a pale grayish green that fills the needs here. The body material should be one of the more absorbent acrylics. Nylon yarn would answer for this. Build the body on the same general lines as the nymph, but more slender if possible, particularly as pertains to the abdomen.

Wings: Two long narrow hackle tips, white saddle is preferred, and dyed very lightly in Putnam's silver gray-green dye. This one may defeat you because Putnam's dye is not always available on the West Coast; however, it seems to be available over most of the Midwest and the East. The wings should be laid flat on top of each other, extending about a quarter-inch longer than the body.

Legs: Hackle wound in front of the wing, and use a very soft wet-fly quality. Use a size eight hackle on a #6 and a size ten on a #8. When folded back, the hackle should not cover more than half of the body.

On streams, and mainly the slow meandering type, fish this fly in the film almost like an emergent nymph but with very little action.

On reedy lakes, cast it close to the reed fields, but still in open water, and try to cast to bulging fish. This way little action is necessary because the fish strikes almost at once, provided, of course, said fish is headed in the right direction when the fly alights on the water.

This Wet Green Damsel is not a standard pattern and you cannot buy it anywhere except in the store I supply in my home town, but be assured it is a highly effective pattern.

Much more could be recorded on the many damsels here in the West, but it would appear the various genera are very localized in their habitat (I know of a tan-and-gold-winged species on Idaho's Silver Creek, and a giant mottled tan-and-gray one on the upper Klamath River) so that with those already listed prevalent on all western waters and always effective, it would seem superfluous to list any more.

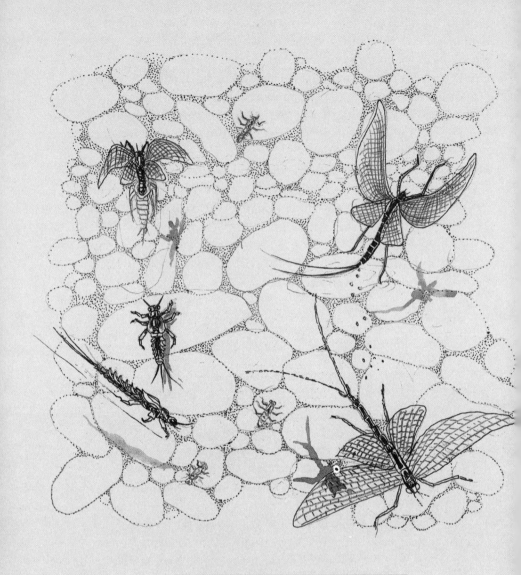

Mayflies
(Order Ephemeroptera)

After forty-five years of fly tying, I still approach this order with some trepidation. There are so many genera of mayflies—well over the three-hundred mark—that it would take the study and writing of a lifetime for anyone to cover them all. However, here in the western states it would seem possible to boil down such an incredible list to a selection based on size, color, and conformation to the point where less than a dozen simulations would suffice for most needs throughout a full season.

This means, of course, that several of the nymph patterns must be tied on hooks ranging from 3XL #6 to 3XL #14 or #16. For example, consider my latest original fuzzy nymph, the Near Enough. This nymph is my twenty-fifth, and it could be called the "Caboose"; certainly it is the end of the train. But it has proven versatile, and is simulative of perhaps six or more mayflies so that it is tied on 3XL hooks varying from #8 to #16. The adults of all of these sizes will be at least one size smaller, and this matter of comparative sizes between the aquatic stages and the adults of all orders will be given a complete treatment in a later chapter.

Great Western Leadwing
(Isonychia velma)

This giant among the mayflies is entirely indigenous to the western states, and it comes to mind first, primarily because I managed to live with it for forty years before discovering it. But then it is a very rare occurrence for anyone to see it after emergence due to its habit of hatching after 9:00 P.M., and that is after legal fishing hours, at least in a lot of western states.

My encounter came about this way. A friend and I were up on the headwaters of the Williamson River fishing the Big Yellow May, *Hexagenia limbata*. After a banner evening we had over a mile walk back to the car. As usual, when the spinner fall occurs with the *limbata,* inside of a few minutes all activity ceases, as if you had turned off a faucet.

The moon lacked about three days to full, so it wasn't bad walking, though at times the road wound in and out of a heavy jack pine forest, and then it was guess and be-Gawd.

When we were about a hundred yards from the car and were passing a big pool, the river suddenly blew up—literally. Big fish were everywhere, tearing the river apart.

"Jim," I yelled, "something else is emerging; I'm going to try to catch one on the Yellow May. Too dark for them to be color conscious, and it has to be big to stir up such an orgy." To make a long story short, I quickly hooked and landed a rainbow of two pounds, the largest of the evening. I also landed a bucketful of moss he was buried in, but no matter; I had, I hoped, a specimen of what I thought had triggered this wild orgy of feasting.

As soon as we arrived at home, this last fish was dissected—and it was really a glutton. It was packed full of Yellow May nymphs, duns, and spinners, but standing out like a sore thumb was a giant nymph of a deep maroon-brown color. Counting its three half-inch tails, it was an easy inch and a half long.

Now at this time, I had never heard of the *velma,* though I had had an acquaintance with a close relative, the *Isonychia bicolor,* for many years, and it was to be found on the lower river. But I did know it was an *Isonychia,* a free swimmer and predator, and thus should be very important to my growing list of originals. All this happened in mid-July and I had only to wait till late August when I attended the Federation of Flyfishers' Conclave at Sun Valley, Idaho, for Ernie Schwiebert's positive identification that my new bug was an *Isonychia velma.*

"You are most fortunate," said Ernie. "Not many of us ever gain a speaking acquaintance with this one."

Tying the *Isonychia velma* Nymph

This being a very active full-time swimming nymph and close to emergence all through the month of July, it would seem best to tie it to be fished in the film. Tying it so has been highly effective.

Hook: #8, 4XL, and either regular-weight wire or 1XF, if available.

Tying Thread: Brownish maroon.

Tails: Three flues from a dark-brown-dyed church window from the ringneck pheasant.

Ribbing: Fine copper wire.

Body: Maroon-brown mohair or a comparable yarn in fuzzy acrylic, left in the round with very little taper at the rear and should be a scant three-sixteenths inch in thickness, but a bit fuller in the thorax.

Legs: Six fibers applied underneath of the same dark brown church window, about one-half inch long.

Gills: Brownish purple maribou, tied on top, which should reach almost but not quite to the rear end of the body. They are left loose for maximum action when swimming the nymph with very short, fast jerks of the rod tip.

You who tie only for yourselves or a friend or two may prefer Ernie Schwiebert's style of applying the gills: bind the maribou down on each side with the copper wire, then pick it out between the segments. This produces an outstanding nymph, though it takes up a little too much of my time.

Wing Cases: Purple-dyed duck-wing coverts, and they simply cap and cover half of the maribou gills. It bears repeating that I never tie down the back of any wing cases, preferring that they be able to flutter in the current to simulate the emerging insect.

Head: Should be built up rather large, then flattened with your pliers.

I fish the *velma* all through June and July—it seems to have no set time to be most effective. I remember another trek to the upper river only last season, when I expected to intercept the Black Drake (*Siphlonurus occidentalis*) hatch. Unfortunately, I was too late. It was all over and only mid-June, and no stream can appear so dead and totally fishless as it is right after this blizzard hatch is over and the trout have so gorged themselves that they seem to go into a state of hibernation till the next hatch starts. There wasn't an insect on the wing, unless you count a stray mosquito or two, so now was a prime time to test out the *velma* nymph.

Now when that brownish maroon body is submerged, it disappears completely, so it became necessary to watch for the belly flash of a turning fish in order to connect on the strike.

I found a deep pool with an undercut bank on the far side, and just like forty-some years earlier, I flipped the nymph onto the far bank, rolled it into the water, and started swimming it across and downstream. That day I proved that the *velma* is a real killer because I caught nine trout of eight inches to a foot in length in less than thirty minutes. All this at 2:00 P.M. on a hot, sunny day.

There seems little point in giving a description of the dun or spinner of this genus, inasmuch as I know of only one emergence where one was collected, and this only on account of a fluke in the weather.

Andre Puyans was on California's famous Hat Creek some years ago on a misty day marked by a drizzle and a heavy dark overcast, so that it seemed the *velmas* mistook it for dusk, and there was a heavy emergence. Here is the description Andy gave me; if you care to add it to your collection just in case, you might be lucky sometime and experience the same set of circumstances.

Hook: #8, 3XL, and fine wire.
Tying Thread: Same as for the nymph.

Tails: Two flues from the dark brown church window, not over a half-inch long. All *Isonychia* have shorter, thicker tails than any other genus of the mayfly order.
Ribbing: Lemon yellow.
Body: Burgundy wine color. The body on all *Isonychia* tends to be a bit obese, always more so than the majority of mayflies.
Wings: Natural black neck-hackle tips at least three-quarters of an inch long.
Legs: Here is the capper: Believe it or not, the hackle or legs are chartreuse, a yellowish-green color.

I can't help but think they need all that contrast so they can find each other in the dark.

Great Leadwing Drake
(Isonychia bicolor)

It would seem that environment can play a big part in the evolution of the species, and it becomes most evident when we compare the eastern *bicolor* with our western version. First, ours is much larger, and more portly overall. Second, the legs on the adult (the spinner) are not cream in the rear and dun in front; rather, they are all a deep grayish dun with all segments a bright yellow.

The dun I have never seen. This could be explained by the fact that the stretch of the Williamson where most of the local hatch occurs is heavily bordered by brush and timber, and since the nymphs emerge in the shallows close to shore, they may stay in this thick cover till they molt into the spinner.

Then everything changes, and you see what looks like a Chinese junk floating on the water at full sail. We have two other mayflies that are larger, both *Hexagenias,* but in the gloaming with reflections lighting up the river and coupled with its giant soot-colored wings, the *bicolor* spinner is something to see. Apparently the trout think so, too, because

The Fuzzy Nymphs of E. H. "Polly" Rosborough

Green Rockworm	Light Caddis Emergent	Dark Stone Nymph
Green Caddis Adult, Wet Version	Light Caddis Adult, Wet Version	Dark Stone Adult, Wet Version
Green Caddis Adult, Dry Version	Light Caddis Adult, Dry Version	Golden Stone Nymph
Little Brown Stone Nymph	Dark Caddis Emergent	Golden Stone Adult, Wet Version
Little Brown Stone, Dry Version	Dark Caddis Adult, Wet Version	Golden Stone Adult, Dry Version
Little Yellow Stone Nymph	Dark Caddis Adult, Dry Version	
Little Yellow Stone Adult, Fore and Aft (Female)		

The Fuzzy Nymphs of E. H. "Polly" Rosborough

Isonychia velma Nymph	Black Drake Nymph	Big Yellow May Nymph
Muskrat Nymph		
Tan Midge Pupa	Black Drake Spinner	Big Yellow May, Spinner
Red Midge Pupa	Black Drake, Spent	Yellow May, Spent
Black Midge Pupa		
Mosquito Larva	Near Enough Nymph	Great Leadwing Drake Nymph
Casual Dress Nymph	Near Enough, Dry Version	Great Leadwing Spinner
Fledermouse		
	Yellow Drake Nymph	Nondescript Nymph
Blonde Burlap		March Brown Hackle
	Yellow Drake Spinner	
Freshwater Shrimp		Green Damsel Nymph
Hare's Ear Nymph	Yellow Drake Hackle	Green Damsel Wet (Immature)

I have seen five-pound rainbows charge ten feet across the current to engulf a big *bicolor.*

Tying the Leadwing Nymph

Hook: #8, 3XL, #38941 by Mustad.
Tying Thread: Henna, a reddish brown.
Tails: Three reddish brown church-window fibers.
Ribbing: Fine copper wire. I prefer the copper wire of late years because you can get eight segments without it appearing too flashy to the fish.
Body: A fiery brown yarn, medium dark, but not too much so because all yarns darken somewhat when wet, though they also tend to brighten as well.
Legs: Fibers from the same feather as the tail.
Gills: Maribou, the same color as the body. This does not correspond to Schwiebert's eastern version, but I took the time to screen out and examine a number of *bicolor* nymphs last May and their coloring was almost static throughout, a rich fiery brown.
Wing Case: Now I wouldn't want anyone to get into *durance vile* by using an illegal feather, but a brown-dyed shoulder-cape feather from the rear of a jungle-cock neck is, by and large, the best wing case available for this nymph. Reason: If you use a waterproof brown marking pencil to color the feather, you do not dye the center quill, so if the wing case covers the front half of the body, you simulate the light median line down the back of the *bicolor*.

So you don't have any old legal jungle cock? A fair substitute is the upper neck feathers from a light Brahma hen, which may be colored in the same way as the jungle-cock shoulder without dying the center quill.

Head: Should be broad and flat, the same as for the *velma*.

Tying the Leadwing Drake, Dry Version

Writing about this big beautiful mayfly is pure pleasure. After forty-five years of study, devising newer and better simulations and still striving for improvement, I feel like we are old friends. But it was not always thus. In the first few years, I had not advanced enough to realize that a fly floating on the stream ten or more feet away, and at twilight as well, can look totally different in the hand, and I fished what I thought was an accurate pattern.

I caught fish, good fish, up to five pounds on my offerings, but still, active feeders would bypass my flies three to one in favor of the nearby naturals.

At that time, I was relying on a #8 Grey Wulff or something similar of my own design, as Lee Wulff had not yet originated his Wulff series of big drys. So finally, in desperation, I stalked the real bug to find out where I was going wrong.

This was easier said than done. You simply do not go catch a great leadwing—you have to let it come to you. But once the proper approach occurred to me, it was ridiculously easy. I simply stood still in the current and when I spotted a fly floating directly to me I bent over with my hand cupped in the water and let the fly float into it.

I was amazed at how dissimilar it was to a Grey Wulff. For one thing, *Isonychias* are badly shorted by nature when it comes to their tails. For such a big insect, which requires a minimum #8 1XLF hook, the tails seem all out of proportion—only a scant half-inch long. They are sturdy insects though.

Earlier, in discussing this big drake, I mentioned the two-color legs; the body is a clear burgundy wine color with bright yellow segments. Wings are three-quarters of an inch

The Great Leadwing Spinner showing the sheared yellow hackle.

high and the head is a golden brown. Following is the complete nomenclature for tying the spinner of this species:

Hook: #8, 1XLF. Anywhere but the West Coast it would be advisable to reduce the size to a #10 1XLF.

Tying Thread: Golden brown.

Tails: Eight or ten flues from a stiff saddle hackle dyed a purplish dun, three-eighths inch long.

Ribbing: Bright yellow nylon thread, at least eight turns.

Body: A rich wine-colored yarn, tied thicker overall than most any other mayfly.

Wings: Two hackle tips from a natural-black cock neck. These may be spent or tied with the concave sides facing each other, inasmuch as you see only one wing unless they

*The finished Great Leadwing (*Isonychia bicolor*).*

are spent. But this rarely happens because the mating hatch takes place at night and all are gone by daylight, though I have fished a spent wet with good success, even when the spinners were floating by.

Hackle: Here we have a problem: how to put yellow joints in purple dun legs. If you follow me, it is easy. With the fly finished except for applying the hackle and head, do this: take a bright yellow saddle hackle completely web-free and reverse the flues. Now shear it off to three-sixteenths of an inch on each side. Wind three turns behind the wings and then three in front. Now wind the same number of turns of stiff purple dun hackle in front and back of the wings, build up a fairly large head, tie off, lacquer, and you have a dry that is a killer in its season. Here on the Williamson this is all during the month of July on any hot evening.

Big Yellow May
(Hexagenia limbata)

Here again we seem to run into the fact that environment, types of water, and so on, can influence not only size in a species, but color as well. I would say that our *limbatas* are very close to the size of the great Michigan caddis (which is, of course, a misnomer because, local name or not, they are all mayflies, not caddis).

But color is a different story. Whereas in the East and Midwest they are called the Great Olive-Winged Drake, out here in the West we call them the Big Yellow May. And they are a bright yellow in the spinner stage. If one wants to be precise, you could say the wings of the dun have a faint pale olive tinge, but I consider that nit-picking. They are yellow, no less.

Here on my home waters, the Yellow Mays make their first appearance right after July fourth, and given hot evenings, this emergence continues all during the month.

Being a burrower in the mud and marl of a stream or lake bottom in the shallows, and the nymphs not being available to the trout until actual emergence, a major hatch can be nothing less than frantic not only for the emergent insects but to the fish and the fisherman. Everything takes place in an hour, never more than ninety minutes, and then one would think the stream and all in it had died, unless that one in a million chance happens and you run into a *velma* hatch on the way home like Jim and I did some years ago.

To prepare for this short period of frantic activity, I make up three leaders—all nine feet in length with the first one to be used with the nymph tapered to three-pound-test at the tippet. The second leader is the same with the dun attached. By this time, when you have some fifteen minutes of fishing time left, it is too dark for the diameter of the leader to be important, so this third terminal gear has a five-pound-test tippet. This bit of preparedness allows you to change leaders fast in the dusk. You can't do this quick-change act if you use a nail knot to attach your leader to the line, and this is the reason I always use a jam knot, which I can simply push apart and then rejam the next leader. With the Yellow May's explosive but short term of emergence, it pays to be ready to change your offering as fast as possible.

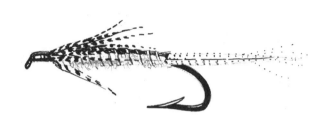

Tying the Big Yellow May Nymph

Hook: #8, 4XL regular weight; a 3XL #6 can be substituted.
Tying Thread: Bright yellow nylon; leave six inches of tying thread trailing for the ribbing.
Tails: One-half-inch-long lemon wood-duck fibers or comparable dyed mallard. If you have lemon wood duck, it needs no dyeing for the tail.
Body: Bright yellow Dazzle-Aire; taper the body slightly its full length. Leave plenty of room for the legs, wing cases, and head. (Remember when you were tying your first hundred or so flies? There was never any place left for the wings and head. We all did it.) The feather used to cap the body should be a shade darker than the tails; a mixture of two parts tan to one part gold Rit—and not too strong—on a mallard flank feather will bring out the proper color. This capping feather is tied in by the tips in front of the tail. It

should be plenty wide enough to cover all of the body's top and a bit down the sides.

Legs: Barred teal dyed in the same color bath, attached beneath at front of body.

Gills: Here is something of a new procedure: Use a small bunch of the same feather as used for the legs and tie this down on top of the body in a flat position reaching almost but not quite to the rear of the body.

Wing Cases: A small duck shoulder feather with circular black barring. Teal, pintail, gadwall, and several other ducks have such feathers and these should be left in the dye bath to gain a deeper shade so they contrast with all other phases of the nymph. The wing cases should cover half the length of the gills.

Head: Big, and flattened as broad as possible. If you want to be super perfect on this nymph, give the dorsal top of the head a coat of light brownish-gold enamel.

Fished in the film from sundown until the duns are prevalent and the trout are splashing instead of bulging, this nymph is a real producer.

Tying the Big Yellow May Spinner

It seems almost pointless to include the dun stage on this mayfly, since the only difference I can detect is in the wings. In the dun they tend to be slightly opaque and with the aforementioned faint olive tinge, so we will concentrate on the spinner, both upright and spent.

Hook: #8, 3XL, #38941 by Mustad. A fine-wire hook would float better but none this length and size are available that I know of.

Tying Thread: Same as for the nymph.

Tail: Several lemon wood-duck flues at least one inch long.

Ribbing: Same as tying thread.

Body: The same bright yellow Dazzle-Aire, and ribbed with at least eight segments. I find no real need for the capping back feather on the adult, though it must be admitted its

The Big Yellow May Dry with tail, ribbing, and body yarn tied in.

The Big Yellow May Dry body with wings and two hackles attached.

The finished Yellow May Dry. The two hackles are interwound front and back a minimum of ten times.

addition will produce a more beautifully finished fly.

Wings: May be varied: white or cream neck-hackle tips dyed a faint yellow, or polar bear dyed in the same color. In either type of wing, they may be tied either upright or completely spent. If polar bear is used, make the wings quite sparse because you are more or less simulating the veining—the wings on the spinner are almost transparent.

Legs: Hackle blended of two web-free saddle hackles, one of bright yellow and one of variegated light ginger or pale olive.

Head: Leave the head round on this one and no dorsal head cap.

The Black Drake
(Siphlonurus occidentalis)

This genus is the very first mayfly I came in contact with in June of 1922—this was also my first year of introduction to fooling the trout. I am bemused, when I think back on those early years, as well as amazed that any of us ever caught any trout, and mostly browns at that, which are supposed to be smarter than any other trout.

The first three years I fished with nothing more than gut leader with two dropper loops that must have tested six pounds at least, and gut-snelled wet flies by Allcock at two for a quarter. Of course, I didn't know that browns were smarter than rainbows or brookies, so by guess and by chance I caught trout. Lots of them, in fact, because with a twenty-five-a-day limit on, seven days of the week, if you didn't produce for a bunkhouse fish fry you didn't share in the Dago Red to wash them down.

Our terminology matched our terminal tackle in sophistication. No one knew a Black Drake as such; we called anything the trout ate a "fly," though if we could buy a reasonable facsimile like a Blue Upright, we called the Black Drake a hatch of Blue Uprights. Simple, wasn't it? Too bad they are not like that now.

This big mayfly is no doubt the most widespread, and produces the greatest hordes of aquatic insects on this continent. I encountered a hatch on our local Long Creek some years ago that one would have to see to believe. There was a solid blue cloud for two hundred feet above the creek and a hundred yards on each side. A friend was with me and when we stepped out of the car we found we didn't dare talk or we would be chewing a hundred drakes. You could easily have slapped two slices of bread together and had a ready-made mayfly sandwich. For two weeks afterward I was blowing dried drakes out of the heater and defroster with the fan.

As mentioned much earlier in this work, the Black Drake Nymph was the second of my original ties, first done about

1933, give or take a year or two. (You will note it took me eleven years to make the great leap from garden hackle into the future.) Actually, the first version has changed but little over the ensuing years. Discovering my felting method with furs and other materials, and adding the noodle to spin the body has been about the only improvement in this pattern.

Emergence dates in the West may vary from May 25 to July 15 depending on the elevation and latitude. Full emergence generally occurs from 10:00 A.M. till late evening, so the angler has a lot of hours to fish the nymph, dun, spinner, and spent during these hours.

Tying the Black Drake Nymph

Hook: Size #10, 3XL, #38941 by Mustad.
Tying Thread: Lead gray nylon or Monocord.
Tail: Four to six flues of finely barred guinea-hen body feather, half an inch long. I prefer all nymph-tail material to be on the soft side. It will give more action in the water.
Body: Fur for the noodle may be of various kinds and blends, such as silvery muskrat or beaver belly. Add to this about twenty percent jackrabbit back fur as a binder and you have the best. Just pull out and discard all the guard hairs from the jackrabbit. (This same blend is also used for tying the Muskrat.) If your wife has a pale Maltese cat, you have a constant source of supply. Of course, both your wife and the cat will hate you, but everyone knows we fly tyers must have grist for our mill. All cat fur makes very fine nymphs.

Proceed the same in tying as for the Muskrat Nymph,

but use an excess of cement under the body, also make the body thicker at the front third or thorax. After scoring it with the hacksaw blade, use a pair of smooth-jawed chain-nosed pliers and flatten the body its full length. Leave plenty of room for the head on all mayfly nymphs because they all have rather large heads.

Legs: Black Drake legs should be slanted slightly back and downward, and use a minimum of five filaments on each side. Legs should be five-sixteenths of an inch long.

Of many different feathers tried for these legs, it seems the finer-barred guinea-hen body feathers are the best.

Wing Cases: Six or eight natural grayish black ostrich flues. You may cut these off square or clip them off with the fingernails. Leave them about three-sixteenths of an inch long and flared a bit wider than the thorax.

Finish off the head half again as long as the normal fly head on a fly of this size. After the half-hitches or whip-finish and before cutting the thread, flatten the head as much as possible. Give the tying thread a bit of a pull, just in case the flattening loosened up anything. Cut the thread and coat the head with clear cement. Later, when it's dry, give it a second coat.

All nymphs described in this book, with the exceptions of those specifically mentioned, are to be fished shallow, at the emergence stage; hence, all have wing cases much darker than the bodies. This is the way nature endowed the naturals. I tied nymphs for nearly fifteen years before I stumbled onto this fact. I caught a lot of fish too, but one time when I was out of gray ostrich, I used some natural black on two of them.

Fishing Oregon's famous Crescent Creek for browns during the early stages of the Black Drake hatch, a couple of fishing pals picked out these two mavericks, "Just to be different," they said. Now neither of them was familiar with the stream. I was, and had fished it over a period of many years. Furthermore, I was conceited enough to believe that I was a better nympher. But they literally hung my hide on the fence for the next several hours. They not only caught more fish, but also bigger fish. The pupils gave the teacher a frustrating day. That night I searched every treatise I owned for the answer and finally found it. The wing cases on all nymphs darken shortly before emergence occurs. This does not mean all are brown, black, or gray. But it does follow that a tan nymph will have brown wing cases, silvery gray ones will have them a dark gray, and nymphs of dark gray or brown will have them almost black in color.

Tying the Black Drake Dun, Spinner and Spent Versions

It may be well to consider the hackle to be used on this dry first, inasmuch as it requires a special dye job to achieve the right color. It is best described as a rusty purplish dun. Philippine white or cream saddle is the first choice for all dyed hackle in the #8 to #14 range; Indian would be second choice. The qualities are relative, but the Philippine feathers average longer, so long in fact, that you can sometimes get two flies from one saddle.

Start your dye procedure with a weak solution of a tan Rit; remove the hackle when it is the color of a brown paper bag when wet. Put the rusty effect in first—you can't do it later.

Remove the saddle and rinse in clear, warm water. Now make a medium-strong solution of gray Rit, bring it to a boil, toss in the hackle, and shut off the heat or you may scald and ruin it. When it is a deep gray, add a small amount of purple, never very much as this is the strongest of all dyes and a little goes a long way. When dark enough, with a dun purple cast, remove the hackle and rinse in a wire-screen strainer till the cold water comes out clear.

Pull one hackle through a paper napkin, then dry high over a gas burner, waving it constantly. As stated previously, it should have a bronze overcast on a dark gray-purple dun base.

Complicated, yes, but what a joy to see your finished Black Drake spinner out there floating on the stream's bosom and find it hard to pick yours out from the naturals all around it. The trout can't tell the difference, either.

While you are about it, use the same dye baths to dye that part of a white or cream neck that will furnish a host of hackle-tip wings for all stages of this drake's forms—duns, spinners, and spents.

While I over-hackle a lot of my duns and leave off the wings, I know there are many who feel a dry doesn't look natural without some semblance of wings, so use them if you insist.

Hook: #8 and #10, 1XL and 1XF (Wright & McGill's #60) is perfect for this fly in both sizes. It is an Improved Sproat semi-forged and is not brittle like most full-forged hooks. While the #8 is closer to the actual size of the natural, it does not float as well as the #10, so most of my commercial ties go on the #10 because it sells better.

Thread: Dark gray and use it for the rib. The head is black, but it is easier to enamel the head black later than it is to cut and tie in gray ribbing.

Tails: A half-dozen flues from the stiff side of the neck hackle. They should be five-eighths of an inch long.

Body: Three-ply nylon yarn, and here we go to the dye pot again. No commercial yarn is produced in the right color for our needs. The three-ply nylon is called "baby yarn"; buy it in white for dying. Nylon is not hard to dye, it just requires more dye and a longer immersion to get the color one needs.

Dye it golden brown first, rinse it out well, and put in a bath of weak purple. You might have to strengthen it before you get the right color, which, when dry, is a purplish brown but only medium dark.

The body is built rather slender and well tapered its full length. Segments should total at least eight. If you elect to tie the dun sans wings, do it with an extra-long saddle hackle. Some of these will give you eight turns, and will it float!

Wings: For the winged spinners and spents, use the hackle tips, and for the #8, five-eighths of an inch long. For the #10 use a half-inch. They can be full upright or semi-spent for the spinner and full-spent for the dead version. On this last one, I shear all hackle from under the thorax, then comes what I term a two-tone job. Enamel the entire back black as well as the head. Then, on the spent, work the black lacquer into the underside of the thorax you sheared. The thorax is always black on the Black Drake. Of course, on the dun and upright spinners, the thorax is covered by the hackle.

It is a fact that the entire series of the drake, nymph, dun, spinner, and spent should be illegal in the hands of our top fly casters; that is, unless they are restricted to full barbless hooks. The flies are that good.

The Yellow Drake
(Unclassified)

While this mayfly is widespread all up and down the West Coast, it seems to have been somehow missed when various entomologists have written on aquatic trout stream insects native to the West.

After researching every treatise I have on the subject, this mayfly would seem to belong in the *Ephemera* genus. I base this conclusion on its habitat, the nymph being a gravel burrower, as well as on the adult's conformation and habit of emergence. Except for its color and slightly smaller size, it appears to be almost identical to the Black Drake. Even its season of emergence is the same, only the hours are different. Whereas the Black Drake may emerge from 10:00 A.M. till almost dark, the Yellow Drake appears at about a half hour before sunset, and as soon as they appear, if there are also Black Drakes available, they will be ignored in favor of the yellow ones. Either the Yellow Drake is a tastier morsel or the trout are ready for dessert after digesting several stomachfuls of Black Drakes all day.

Tying the Yellow Drake Nymph

Hook: #10, 3XL, #38941 by Mustad.
Tying Thread: Pale yellow, sometimes called maize. Leave five inches of the working thread trailing to use for the rib.
Tails: Lemon wood duck a full half-inch long.
Body: Pale cream Dazzle-Aire. Use the "baby" size on this so the body will not be too fat; it should be slender and well tapered. After ribbing, the body may be flattened or left in the round, but if left in the round, the head should still be flattened.
Legs and Wing Cases: Lemon wood duck; the butts of the legs are pulled back and overwound to create the wing cases in the same manner as on the Little Stone. Clip off the butts about three-sixteenths of an inch back from the head; build up the head, flatten it, lacquer, and the nymph is ready to go.

Tying the Yellow Drake Spinner

There seems to be little difference between the dun and the spinner in this species and with only a hour's time to fish it, it seems unnecessary to include the dun. Either version produces well for its full hour of appearance. And, since you have just tied the nymph, it is ridiculously easy to tie the spinner.

Hook: #10, 1XL and 1XF (Wright & McGill #60).

Tying Thread: Maize, same as for the nymph.

Tails: A bit longer than on the nymph, but of the palest honey-colored hackle flues. This drake has only two tails, so do not use more than is necessary to support the rear of the fly on the water.

Ribbing: Identical to the nymph.

Body: Same yarn as for the nymph. The body is, of course, smaller and more delicate than the nymph, but the conformation is the same.

Wings and Legs: Both are of the same color; if you are lucky enough to own one of Metz's extra-pale natural blue dun necks, you are all set. If not, you go back to the dye pot and use pure white hackle for the job. A weak solution of Rit gray will get the right pale gray in very little time in the dye bath. Always remember: wet material is several shades darker than when dry, and one feather is far paler than when in a bunch or on a neck.

You can put hackle-tip wings on this one, upright or spent, but it will not catch any more fish than will a straight hackle. In any case, when winding the hackle, don't wind it close together. Let it spread a bit so as not to create too much color contrast with the body. When dispensing with the wings, I have even half-palmered the front half of the body to keep the color contrast down to the minimum.

The Nondescript Nymph

This one is truly a simulation of many different species of nymphs. In the main, it is intended to represent several of the mayfly nymphs known as the stone clingers, or rock sprawlers. There are many varieties of these distributed all over North America. You will find them clinging tightly to the undersides of rocks or anywhere else they can hide. They are always flat, with dark brown, brown-mottled, or olive-brown to almost all-black backs. Their undersides may vary widely: tan, dirty yellow to off white, but so far a two-tone job has not been found necessary for the simulation. However, with the advent of the new waterproof marking pens, it is very easy to come up with fine two-tone markings. Just tie the body the color of the belly, then mottle the back to the desired color with the marking pen.

The one reason for the shape of these stone clingers is their habitat and the fact that they are all fast-water nymphs. When flattened against the underside of a rock, they meet with the least possible resistance from the stream flow. They are always upside down.

The original idea of the Nondescript I cannot claim as my own. Rather, it is the brainchild of Jim "Red" Chase, formerly of this area but now retired and living in Portland, Oregon. Jim was an avid fly fisherman while living on the Williamson and his agile brain stood him in good stead when he became an amateur fly tyer. One day he brought me a sample of the Nondescript, though its naming actually came a year later when its worth was beyond doubt.

"I've been slaughtering the fish on this bug," Jim said, "and big ones, too. One this morning weighed eight pounds." That was enough for me. I sat right down and tied two of them with a bit of variation in the hackling just to see which was best. I still don't know, and that has been twenty years ago; they both work equally well.

Trying to correlate this nymph with all of the various genera it can be tied to imitate would take up far too much space, so I will settle for one family, and that is all of the browns and mottled browns, both light and dark, of the extensive family Heptageniidae. And out of the galaxy of species in this large family, I have selected the *Stenonema vicarium,* our American March Brown, as being the most representative, both in coloration and size, to the present version of the Nondescript. There are many and good reasons for settling on this genus, including size, and in cases where it is warranted, colors. But in the final result, you should always end up with the same assembly and conformation.

Tying the Nondescript Nymph

Hook: You have great latitude here on hook size and lengths, but my personal choice is a #10 3XL, 2XS Sproat #1206 by Wright & McGill and available only from Buz's Fly Shop in Visalia, California 93277.
Tying Thread: Medium-brown nylon, sometimes called seal brown.
Tail: Three flues from a center tail feather of the cock ringneck, or in my case, I prefer a quarter-inch fluff of fiery brown marabou. Maribou actually gives you more swimming action than any other material.
Ribbing: Bright yellow nylon.
Body: Deep fiery brown synthetic yarn, the fuzzier the better. Start the body in front where you want it to end and fatten it up at the start or at least a third of the way to the rear. The idea is to end up with a flat body that looks like a narrow wedge of pie. Use an excess of glue, both under and between the two layers, so that when flattened and dry it will be a solid melded unit. When starting the return wrap, make one turn, then, with the yarn, tie in the tip of a long web-free fiery furnace saddle hackle. Try to finish the body with a

strong taper from the rear all the way to the front. When the body is finished, flatten it as much as possible. Again, it should look like a narrow wedge of pie; all of the *Stenonemas* have this characteristic shape.

Now wind the ribs three thirty-seconds apart. That sounds like nit-picking, but in this case it is important because the hackle is wound right in the middle between the ribs, and the spacing of the rib gives you about seven to eight segments on a 3XL hook.

The finished body of the Nondescript Nymph ready for palmering.

The hackle in place and ready to be sheared.

Your saddle hackle should be long enough to allow three extra turns at the front wound tight together.

Tie off with a large flat head and fill it with cement while building it. Flatten it well before cutting your thread. All *Stenonemas* have broad flat heads.

Now your bug requires a haircut. Hold the bend of the hook between thumb and forefinger with the eye facing you. With a very sharp scissors, shear the hackle from one-quarter inch long in front down to zero in front of the tail. Be careful—don't include the tail. It is easy to do. Shear it all the way

The finished Nondescript Nymph.

around evenly so the finished job looks like a cone, as in the photo.

Earlier I mentioned that the first two Nondescripts tied were somewhat different in appearance and that I could detect no difference in their effectiveness, and now is the time to explain that variance. One was tied as Red tied his; that is, a full bristle of hackle all around, and the other was sheared clean on both top and bottom, leaving the clipped legs or gills only on the sides. I have learned only in the last year or two that this version looks very close to an immature *Isony-*

chia bicolor—so close their own mothers would have trouble telling them apart. This would be in May and June before the *bicolors* have grown their big wing cases.

The Nondescript has many favorable qualities. It simulates a host of fast-water stone clingers when tied in sizes from #8 2XL to #14 3XL. I find it best on regular or 2XS hooks, and there is a cogent reason for this. It is good at any depth at almost any time of the day and from June to late August. What more could one ask? As a rule, I tie mine on #10 3X and 2XS.

When casting, allow this nymph to sink say two feet or more, then start a fast, very short, jerky retrieve. If the fish are feeding, you are in business, and there does not have to be any emergence taking place.

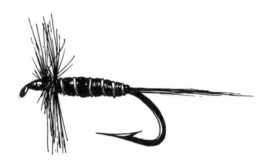

Tying the March Brown, Dun and Spinner Versions

An attempt will be made here to combine several of the myriad March Brown patterns in use at this time. There are English, American, and Canadian, as well as many local versions, all of which overlap.

Two offshoots from the original English March Brown come to mind, though here the names are radically different. These are the old Red Upright and the Red Quill. Both of these flies may be fished wet or dry and with good success when the *Stenonema vicaria* are hatching, but I still lean a bit more to a wingless version of the English March Brown when tying the spinner and hackle-tip wings for the dun.

Our March Browns here in the West tend to hover, when in the spinner state, from six inches to several feet above the water. This causes some spectacular acrobatics on the part of the trout; sometimes a spinner will be taken over a foot above the water. Over fifty years ago on Bear Lake in the Gold Lake Basin of northern California, I watched two- to five-pound brown trout take dragonflies from two feet in the air. Believe me, I caught no fish.

Hook: Sizes may vary from #8 1XL and 1XF to the same hook in #14. All are #60 by Wright & McGill.

Tying Thread: Dark brown nylon.

Tails: Two flues from a center tail feather of a ringneck cock pheasant for the dun, or a wisp of medium-brown stiff web-free saddle hackle for the spinner. The hackle tail will give you a better float. The best body material I have found to date is Acorn Mohlon, but a comparable yarn in any of the new synthetics will do. I prefer it to be fuzzy.

Ribbing: This is a medium amber and if you can soil it a bit so much the better, because it should not be too evident. Belding makes a silk thread in a grayish amber that is perfect if you can find it.

Body: All bodies on this March Brown should have a decided taper.

Hackle: Should be of the best dry-fly quality and fiery brown in color. If you elect to use hackle-tip wings, they should be very sparse because when these flies are hovering you see nothing but their bodies suspended in the air. For this reason alone, the shape, size, and color of the body are all important.

The Near Enough Nymph

Like the preceding nymph, the Nondescript, this last and, I hope, final original does many things. Whereas the first one covers many of the brown nymphs plus the adults, this one does the same thing in the gray spectrum.

The Near Enough, however, has a decided advantage over the Nondescript in that almost all of the grayish nymphs it simulates are swimming nymphs representing several families. This means, of course, that in a full range of sizes—2XL #8 to 3XL #16—they have no particular season, and if fished during a feeding period, have no set hour.

The list of possible simulations is extensive, and all can be tied with the same list of materials, so it would be well at this point to list both the families and genera as follows: family, Baetidae: *Siphlonurus occidentalis*; family, Baetidae: *Isonychia campestris*; family: Baetidae, *Ephemerella excrucians*. The foregoing three species should be enough for one nymph to simulate. All of these are widespread and are also somewhat diverse in their seasons, but only the *Ephemerella excrucians* has a really limited time of access to the trout in that it is not out constantly swimming in the current and thus always vulnerable. That's what I like about the *Isonychia* and *Siphlonurus,* they are always out there challenging the trout.

Tying the Near Enough Nymph

Hook: All 3XL regular-weight Improved Sproat (Mustad #38941), #8 to #16, but there is no reason for you not to try them even smaller.

Tying Thread: Either a very pale lead gray or a pale tannish gray.

Tails, Legs, and Wing Cases: Barred mallard, dyed in a

very weak solution of half gray and half tan Rit. All should be two shades darker than the body. Tails should be from three-eighths to five-eighths of an inch long, depending on the size of the hook.

All bodies are spun of the same type and color of fur: gray fox underfur from the sides and back of the pelt, and be sure to remove all of the guard hair. You don't want any black-and-white tipped guard hair messing up the final result. All bodies are slender and well tapered. There is no special definition of the thorax; the body just thickens there.
Legs: Applied the same as for the Yellow Drake and Little Yellow Stone; that is, you bend the butts of the legs back, overwind them, and create the wing cases, which should be clipped off one-third the length of the body. Leave both body and head in the round on the Near Enough. Most of the swimming nymphs have this form. You can rough up the sides a bit to simulate gills, but even this addition does not seem to enhance its fish-taking qualities; it's a killer any way you look at it.

There will be no attempt to specify any particular dry pattern to accompany the various sizes of the Near Enough. But I will list several possibles, all standard patterns that all of you are familiar with and, no doubt, your fly boxes are well stocked with them already: Quill Gordon, Gray Fox, Blue Quill, Red Quill, Light Hendrickson, Whirling Blue Dun—and the list could go on and on but these should be more than enough to keep you busy.

Midges
(Order Diptera)

To attempt any exhaustive thesis on the order Diptera would require a book in itself, so we will try to keep this discussion down to three or at the most four, the fourth to be one of our most prevalent mosquitoes.

The Black Midge
(Chironomus larva)

This little silver-gray worm tied on a #14, 3XL, #38941 Improved Sproat is in reality the first nymph described in this book. Just spin the noodle of muskrat belly fur, create a very thin segmented body of eight segments, add some six or eight fine-barred guinea flues underneath and in front of thorax as legs, spin a black ostrich head, and of course use black tying thread, and you have a working edition of a *Chironomus* larva that will produce trout anywhere in the world.

This larva should be fished from one to three feet in depth. It is not too effective in the film. While it may be dressed in many body colors, I have found that here in Oregon and in northern California waters the dirty gray body and black head is far and away the most successful pattern. Our most prevalent midge is called the black midge and seems to occur only in cold spring-water streams where water temperatures never exceed fifty degrees. Oddly enough, I have never seen the trout taking the adult of this species, though there will be a major tailing rise for the pupa from daylight till sunrise and another from sundown till deep dusk. And this with thousands of the tiny adults buzzing in swarms only an inch or so above the water's surface.

I strongly suspect there is no protein value to the black midge adult and leave it to the trout to choose their own food, as apparently they do. For instance, has anyone ever seen a trout take a water skater? Either they have no food value or they must just plain taste bad.

The Black Midge Pupa

This member of the midge family is so named because the adult has a black body; however, both the foregoing larva pattern and the pupa are actually a dirty gray and both have black heads, a definite departure from the way most tyers tie them. Also, I tie all midge pupa with the heads and gills at the rear.

If properly assembled by this method they will float with the bend of the hook upright in the film, sea-horse style.

Tying the Black Midge Pupa

Hook: One size only: #12, #38930 XF Improved Sproat by Mustad. On any smaller hook, it floats too high—any larger, it sinks too deep.

Tying Thread: Pale clear gray nylon to match the body color.

Head: Spin three or four black ostrich flues and make three turns right at the hook's bend.

Gills: Now, if you are profligate with your supergrizzly neck hackle, wind three turns of a size sixteen tight up against the head. This small collar simulates the gills. Always wind it convex side forward so the oily side of the hackle will float the bug better. Never use any hackle with the least bit of web.

If you would rather be more frugal, you may shear a stiff web-free saddle hackle down to a width where, when wound, the tips just reach the point of the hook. Out of a long saddle you can get three pupae. The same color of hackle is used on all three midge pupae to be discussed. All should be of the pale spectrum.

Body: Pure Orlon four-ply yarn, and this is split to two-ply so a properly tapered body can be wrapped. Tie in the ribbing thread in front of the gills, then the Orlon. The body and head are of the same color of gray, the rib should be a

A #12 Black Midge Pupa greatly enlarged shows the reverse-style tie.

shade darker so the segments will be evident, and they will be even more so when wet. Need I say "plenty of cement on the hook" now? Wind the body fatter in front of the gills and then taper it fast to the head. Try to get eight segments with the ribbing thread, and here is where 6/0 nylon comes into its own, provided you can get it in the right shade of gray.

As stated earlier, the black midge's habitat is strictly limited by its intolerance to any waters over fifty degrees in temperature. It also follows that its hours of emergence would tend to prove it cannot tolerate bright light because from sunrise to sundown there is never any activity, even with a heavy cloud cover.

So be on your favorite spring stream at daylight, fish till the sun hits the water, go elsewhere till sundown, then fish till dusk. Always fish midge pupae on a dead drift across and downstream. A nine-foot leader tapered to two-and-one-half-pound-test is the best terminal setup I have found yet, and if the fish are tailing, even a tyro can't help but catch some fish. They tend to hook themselves as the fish lie not more than a foot below the surface and wait for the emergers to come to them. Then they simply rise enough to clamp down on the pupa and, as said before, hook themselves.

The Red Midge Pupa

This midge's habitat and hours of emergence are sharply in contrast with the black midge. It will inhabit waters of up to sixty-five degrees and it will emerge all day.

A notable place for this midge is the Upper Sacramento River of northern California and thereby lies a story of a late friend, one Dee Olson. He was born and raised on the river and outside of his working hours as a railroad man spent practically all of his time fishing the Sacramento. He was also a fly purist and used only one size and pattern. This was a #12 wet Gray Hackle with a red body. Forty-five years ago about the only flies available in our local stores were the C-grade of Allcock's wet snelled flies. These sold at two for a quarter and yours truly caught his first trout on one of them; that is, the first on a fly.

Somehow Dee learned that by removing the tinsel ribbing, then singeing off the red tail and outer half of the hackle with a lighted cigarette, he had a consistent killer. None of us suspected he was using a Red Midge Pupa; certainly I didn't, and it was nearly fifteen years later that I became aware of the fact, partly through the evolution of my Black Midge, and the rest from textbooks on aquatic insect life.

Tie this one identically to the Black Midge except for the body colors and the head.

Hook: Same size.
Tying Thread and Ribbing: Crimson nylon.
Body: Also of crimson Orlon or a comparable yarn. Very little contrast is wanted between the body and the rib. What is wanted is evidence of segmentation.

All midge pupa are fished with the same technique, just the habitat and hours will vary.

The Tan Midge Pupa

While entomologically a member of the Diptera order, the tan midge is more properly a big mosquito, the one we generally call the big swamp mosquito. And the female does bite, though their sting seems to be less lethal than that of the little black-and-white variety. They do raise an itching welt but it does not last as long as that of the little black-and-white devils.

So far as I can determine, it is a member of the family Culicidae and is of the *Anopheles* genus. It is very widespread and will be most prevalent in the warmer waters, both swampy-edged streams and especially along lake shores. I can remember being almost eaten alive by these insects along the swampy lower sections of Wood River one late evening.

Tying the Tan Midge Pupa

Hook Size: #10 only, #38930, the same as for the Black and Red Midges, it is just a size larger.
Tying Thread: Palest tan nylon.
Head and Gills: Also the same: just shear the gill hackle wide enough to reach to a #10 point instead of a #12.
Ribbing: Same as the tying thread.
Body: Pale tan fuzzy yarn. A pale beige is the right color.

The rest of the procedure is the same as for the Red and Black versions. Only the colors and the hook are different. Much like the Red Midge Pupa, the tan can be fished at all hours. Sunlight does not seem to bother it.

I can't say I have ever seen a good tailing rise when this pupa was a top producer, but inasmuch as I generally fish it at early evening when the adult females are sucking me dry of blood, this would seem the obvious time to use it; that is, if you can take the punishment. Even Cutters won't stop them entirely.

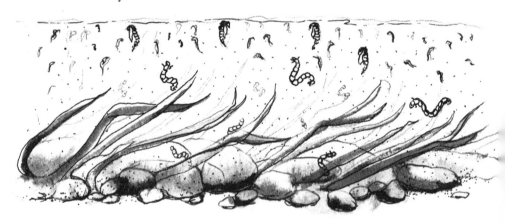

The Mosquito Larva

Family Culicidae, genus would seem to be *Anopheles* also, judging from the larva's habit of swimming in a horizontal position. This is one of the later developments of my original list of twenty-five nymphs. Number twenty-four, in fact, just before the Near Enough. Observing these larvae by the thousands in the backwater overflows of the Upper Williamson was what prompted me to develop this highly productive bug.

Tying the Mosquito Larva

Hook: #14 or #16, #38941, 3XL. In fact, we have used this hook on some eight or ten of the nymphs discussed so far.

Tails: On every guinea hen there are a few dozen feathers that are so finely barred that one has to look twice to define them. All such feathers are reserved for this one nymph. Use three flues three-eighths of an inch long for the tails.

Tying Thread and Ribbing: Are the same, so leave a four-inch trailer when you tie in the tail for the rib.

Body: A smoke gray yarn, about what you would use on a Grey Wulff. It should be two-ply because you want a very slender body with little or no taper. The body is left in the round.

Legs: Six flues from the guinea hen are added underneath for the legs, not more than three-sixteenths of an inch in length.

Head: Gray thread tied a bit thicker than the body, and if you want to be super-authentic, give it a pair of big black eyes on the sides of the head—they are almost as pronounced as those on a damselfly.

I don't know how these larvae act when undisturbed, but when you wade near them they become highly agitated and dart hither and yon much like small minnows. As a consequence of this behavior, I fish them with as short and fast a rod tip agitation as I can, and it must be right part of the time because the Mosquito Larva will really take the trout.

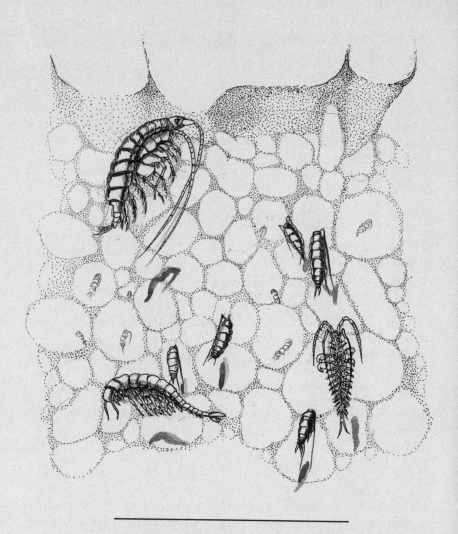

Freshwater Shrimp and Scuds

(Order Amphipoda)

No attempt will be made to classify any of the Amphipoda order as to family or genus, there are simply too many of them and I am on speaking terms with only two or three. Properly speaking, they are not nymphs at all, inasmuch as they spend their entire lives in the water with no emergence to a winged insect. But that does not mean they should not be included in any list of effective nymph patterns.

Tying the Shrimp

Hook: On all sizes and colors of the Amphipoda, I use one pattern of hook and this is entirely due to its shape. This is Mustad's #3906 in #6 to #12. This hook has a quick drop-off at the curve, more like the original Sproat, and all shrimp and scuds have a humpbacked curved carapace. Many tyers bend their hooks more to gain this effect, but in so doing you lose much of the needed bite in the hook gap and miss a lot of strikes.

Tying Thread: Match the body, be it tan, gray, olive, or, in the case of some very cold spring streams, it may be flesh colored. Our local Spring Creek has a big population of this color. Talk about your naked little nymphs!

Tail: The tip of a hackle of the same color as the body. Use them of various widths to fit the hook size. The tail should always be tied well down on the curve of the hook, and the right effect is best obtained with the #3906.

Body: Any of the very fuzzy yarns and the color should come as close as possible to the color of the shrimp or scuds you are simulating in the waters you fish. That could range from pale green to gray. I have never seen a gray shrimp, but years ago when I was tying at the Federation of Fly Fishers Annual Conclave at Jackson Hole, Wyoming, a young boy from the Rio Grande country asked me to tie him a #8 Shrimp and when I started to tie it in the usual tan, he said, "No! No! Our shrimp are the same color as your Black Drake Nymph." In actuality, the finished job looked like a humpbacked Black Drake.

A #8 Shrimp starts with the tail and body material attached.

The body and tail are ready to be palmered with hackle.

The hackle in place and ready for shearing.

The finished #8 Shrimp.

Bodies are started in front as usual. Leave plenty of room for a big well-tapered head. Fatten up the body in front to start with; this will make it easier to get a pronounced taper on the return trip, which adds to the humpbacked appearance.

Legs (Swimmers): On the return trip, tie in the tip of a web-free saddle hackle. It should be of a color as close to that of the body as possible. Tie in the hackle tip after you have made one or even two turns of the yarn on the return trip. This helps to keep the fish's teeth away from the body and your nymph lasts longer. Palmer-wind the hackle with about six or more turns and you should have enough left for two or even three turns close together at the front of the body. Width of this saddle hackle is not too important because you are going to shear off all but that underneath.

Holding it by the curve of the hook and looking toward the eye, shear off all hackle on the top and down the sides. Now reverse your grip; that is, grasp it between the thumb and forefinger, squeeze the hackle underneath tight together and shear if off from three-eighths of an inch in front to zero at the rear. You should always wind up with zero at the rear, but the three-eighths length is based on a #8 hook. On a #6 it will be one-half inch and on a #12 only a quarter inch or less.

Head: All heads should be long and perfectly tapered from the front of the body down to the eye.

I know, of course, that books on tying stress the addition of a hard shellback effect, but I have never found this added time-consuming factor necessary. My versions catch the trout, and, after all, that is the desired result.

A long time ago, perhaps twenty years or more, I embraced a fly-tying motto: "Keep them simple." In this respect I am reminded of the late and great Big Jim Leisenring, author of *Tying the Wet Fly,* in which Big Jim, much like Dee Olson, settled on one basic wet fly for all of his needs: a thin body of bronze peacock with a long soft coch-y-bondhu hackle in front, and almost invariably on a #10 hook. Big Jim's philosophy holds just as well today as years ago. Keep them simple.

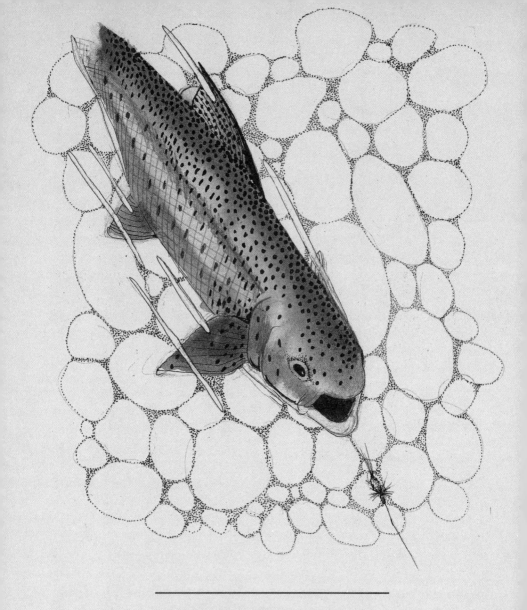

Food Nymphs

This chapter will deal with four nymphs that are intended to simulate general food forms for a hungry trout. One of this group does much the same thing that the shrimp and scud simulations do, so it will be considered first.

The Blonde Burlap

I am told that the original Burlap was the brainchild of the late Arnold Arana of Dunsmuir, California, steelheader par excellence, a real innovator in the tying of steelhead flies for the Klamath River. I do know he gave those who followed him a good foundation to build on. His original version is still just as good as when it was brought out over thirty-five years ago, and it is still fished extensively on many West Coast streams. In some localities it is rather humorously referred to as The Gunnysack Fly, inasmuch as the body is composed of jute unraveled from a gunnysack.

While the original did very well for me, too, I still wanted a variation of my own, and so the Blonde Burlap came into being. As a consequence, I have found the Blonde to be more consistent than the original pattern on big browns in central Oregon's big Wick-i-up Reservoir during the fall run up the Big Deschutes River. I am certain in my own mind that this is because it matches perfectly the color of the shrimp native to these waters. As one might expect, size does not seem important, because I tie it on #2 to #10, and all with good results, as might be expected for a shrimp tie.

Tying the Blonde Burlap

Hook: The one described here is tied on a #6 2XS hook. It may be either a regular length shank or 1XL.
Thread: The lightest tan available, something like a pale beige.
Tail: A short, thick bunch of soft honey dun hackle. Tie it well down on the curve of the hook, shrimp-style.

Body: Three strands of jute from a gunnysack. Taper the strands for the first inch from the end you tie in in front of the tail, then throw a spinning loop to spin the burlap on. Now, in order to get a nice taper, it is necessary to take the tying thread back to a point one-eighth of an inch back of the eye, and there tie in about four inches of two-ply light tan yarn. This can be wool, acrylic, or what-have-you—you are going to cover it up anyway. Taper it well at the rear and also a bit in front. You spin the three strands of jute in the loop and wind the body the same as you would a fur one. Use plenty of cement between the core and the jute outer cover. After you have tied one or two, you will know very close to just how long the jute strands need to be, so taper the front ends to coincide with your last turn so you won't wind up with a big lump at the tie-off.

Legs (Swimmers): There are rooster necks generally available called "honey dun." These are honey color with a light dun center. Choose a wide wet-fly type and wind five or six turns in front of the body. Wind with convex or shiny side in

front, then hold all of it back and overwind it so it will lay back. The flues should be long enough to reach the hook barb. Never trim this collar as we did the palmered shrimp, since this is more or less of a wet spider-type nymph.

In order to get the right shade of burlap for this nymph, it must be bleached. I wash first and then bleach a long strip of burlap in twenty-volume hydrogen peroxide in a glass jar until it is a shade lighter than it was before bleaching and when wet. A strip the length of the average gunnysack and four to five inches wide is ideal to work with. Roll it up into a cylinder and cram it into a jar that will just hold it. Fill the jar with bleach and a half hour later fill it up nearly full again. Never screw the lid down more than one turn or it may blow off. Once the bleach starts action, it will boil over a bit, so set the jar in a shallow pan to catch the overflow.

When you remove it from the jar, do it with a pair of pliers and dump it into a pan of hot soap suds to remove the peroxide. If you get your hands in this twenty-volume, you will wind up looking like a leper. It takes days for the effects to disappear. The dried-out jute will be two shades lighter than the average burlap bag. It seldom takes more than a full day to bleach jute.

After the body is in place, take your piece of hacksaw blade and score the body enough so it is quite rough, but be careful not to cut too deep. Jute is a rather flimsy material, and that is the reason for a base of cement under it. When that cement sets up hard, the burlap will take a lot of beating.

Jute would probably be used a lot more and in many colors if all those tyers who are forever casting about for a material that creates an envelope of air bubbles around it ever immersed a Blonde Burlap and observed what happens to it. In the proper colors, it would be fantastic for the bodies of caddis emergents. Try it. All colors of burlap are now available in fabric shops.

My fly boxes are always well stocked with Blonde Burlaps in several sizes. They nearly always produce, especially when there is little activity among the natural nymphs. For the past fifteen years or more, the Blonde Burlap has been top dog in my fly box on my annual trek to Wick-i-up. This is generally mid-October, and with no fly hatches left at that time, the shrimp simulations seem to be the best.

The Hare's Ear Nymph

I find it hard to define this nymph, larva, pupa—whatever one chooses to call it. Its history goes back to the era before my first nymph. Local anglers had discovered that by taking a wet pattern of Allcock's Hare's Ear, singeing the body down to half its original diameter with a lighted cigarette, than singeing the wings off in a like manner so they were left one-third as long as the body, they had a killer fly for our famous Spring Creek.

Spring Creek boasts of tremendous hatches of black midges, and what is of more importance with reference to the Hare's Ear, it also produces large hatches of a small grayish olive caddis almost neutral in shade. Strangely enough, the trout rarely feed on the adult caddis, and much the same for the black midge although I doubt that it is for the same reason; that is, lack of protein in the adult. Rather, I choose to believe that it is because there are so many pupae available, and they are much easier to get by tailing than by using up the extra energy required to catch the adult. Then again, this food nymph is close enough to a spent dark alderfly in the film so that if both the caddis and alder are in emergence, you are carrying a double-barreled shotgun instead of a single.

Local anglers used the half-burnt-up Allcock's Hare's Ear in the right size, about a #12. Fished in the film the same way

as the Black Midge Pupa, it was a consistent killer. Any time the fish were showing on the surface (that is, tailing), it was an open-and-shut cinch that the Black Midge Pupa or the Hare's Ear, and sometimes both, would produce, as I learned in later years when I was trying both patterns.

When I returned to southern Oregon in the spring of 1936 after nearly four years in northern California, I came back armed with some three or more years of nymph lore, so when a local angler asked for some Hare's Ears, I simply tied them to look like the singed version and we had a new nymph.

Oddly enough, when fished in other waters, we have found it can be tied on most any size hook and still be productive. As a consequence, I tie it on hooks from #6 to #14, and if you are deft enough to get one on the tiny sizes such as #20 and #22, you will be amazed at the number of strikes it will produce.

Tying the Hare's Ear

Hook: #12, regular weight and shank hook #3906 by Mustad.
Thread: Black.
Tail: None.
Body: Use a blend of two parts muskrat belly, one part jackrabbit back for binder (be sure to remove all guard hairs from the rabbit), plus two parts of medium-brown mink. If no mink is available, bleach a piece of the darker muskrat till it is a golden brown. Leave it on the hide while bleaching; otherwise, it will felt and be very hard to blend with the gray furs. You should wind up with a heather mixture of dun. Taper the noodle to the extreme at the rear because the finished body should be thick in front and taper all the way back.
Gills: Leave lots of room in front of the body for a very short collar in one of the various choices here listed: the back fur of a winter-killed packrat (don't snicker, this is one of the best, plus being a top dubbing); flying squirrel back and tail; giant African mole; and, if all else fails, bleach a muskrat belly till it takes on a dun tinge. I have found I can have quite a variance in the furs used for a Hare's Ear collar and all will catch fish. The main requirement seems to be fineness and softness so it works well in the current on a dead drift.

The collar should be spread evenly all the way around the hook and cover the front half of the body. I hold the bunched fur on top of the hook, throw a loose loop around it, then by tightening and then loosening the tension, it practically goes in place automatically. When you go to applying all the materials for this nymph on a small hook, you will understand the reason for allowing plenty of room in front of the body. If you do not, you will soon run out of hook.

Wing Case: The very tops in feathers for the wing cases are the speckled black-and-brown wing feathers from a brown leghorn hen. These may be hard to find now because few of this breed are being raised of late years. However, only two years ago I ran onto a good substitute, and, in fact, you can use the whole bird—well, almost. This is the dark Cornish hen you pay such exorbitant prices for in the more fancy eateries. The Cornish feathers are a bit darker than the leghorn but not too much, and the whole main body is of all the same pattern of dark brown well mottled with black.

Use only a very small bunch of the speckled feather for the wing cases, and they should not be over one-third as long as the body. Also, flare it a bit. Collar the head with three twisted black ostrich flues, finish the head, cement it, and the nymph is finished.

Tied on a heavy #8 hook, this nymph is a sure producer on Oregon's famous Diamond Lake early in the season. One local husband and wife team cruise the shoreline looking for fish spawning in the shallows. They know from past experience that there will be nearly as many bright sterile fish just beyond the spawners waiting for a chance to dart in and steal a few eggs. A big Hare's Ear Nymph cast out as far as possible, and then retrieved in short choppy jerks through the pirates, shrinks their numbers in a hurry. A most versatile nymph, the Hare's Ear.

Fledermouse Nymph

This nymph is probably as near all-purpose as it would

be possible to devise. It must not be confused, however, with the Fledermaus, the creation of the late Jack Snyder of San Francisco, a long-time devotee of Montana's famous Big Hole River. Jack's version was originated to simulate low-flying bats at dusk. He said he had never seen one of the river's giant browns take a bat, but he was certain they did a lot of wishful thinking, seeing all that meat on the wing. And it is history that Snyder's Fledermaus took a lot of the Big Hole's browns. And so would this Fledermouse, and that is one

reason for the different way of spelling it.

With one small exception, my way of tying this nymph is modeled after the pattern pictured in Al McClane's old column in *Field & Stream,* "One for the Book," some twenty or more years ago. (Why did he ever quit writing that goodie? I even made it once.)

Being universal in appeal, the Fledermouse may be tied on almost any size hook from a #2 to a #16, and preferably 2 or 3XL, the weight of the hook being governed entirely by the season and water conditions. It never really simulates anything specific, but its hazy outline allows the fish to think it might be any number of nymph.

Tying the Fledermouse

Tying Thread: A light golden brown nylon. I formerly used Nymo for all of my tying and if you are lucky enough to find any #1248 Turf Tan, grab it. However, there is a fair counterpart made in Monocord available.

Hook: Tie on a #8, 3XL, either regular weight or 2XS.
Tail: None.
Body: So far I have been unable to find a yarn of any kind that will make a satisfactory substitute for the blended furs in use since I first started tying this nymph. Perhaps it is just as well—someone might accuse me of plain laziness.

For the body dubbing, I use the same blend of furs and in the same percentages as used for the Hare's Ear, well tapered at the rear and thick in front. Leave a bit of extra room in front because this one has a fur collar almost identical with the Hare's Ear but of different fur. You could even call it a mini skirt. Don't forget the cement, and rough up the body well with the hacksaw blade. You can't make this one too ragged.

Most all of the big suppliers of fly-tying material now have Australian opossum for sale. This fur is a heather mixture of tans, grays, and brown, well barred and in color much like the old African orange baboon we used to get.

Spin a collar around the front of the body the same way you did for the Hare's Ear. It should cover the front third of the body and you will need to remove about half of the base dubbing or the head will be too big. Don't throw away one smidgen of this fur, not even the butts you cut from the collar. Save it all and later mix it in with the rest of your fur mix to make more body dubbing. If you tie only for your own needs, you can tie all of the body and collar from the possum, but this fur is not as cheap to buy as the blend I use for tying this nymph by the gross.

The wing cases are in two layers and in two colors. Both should be of the same length and cover half of the body; first, a small bunch of barred teal or mallard, topped with a like bunch of brown widgeon. You have no widgeon? Okay, dye some teal golden brown.

Head: Long and tapered up to the body like a shrimp's.

I like this one and a customer of mine from Corvallis, Oregon, uses it almost exclusively. Some years ago, he ordered several dozen nymphs from me and a half dozen were the Fledermouse. He only gets to go fishing about once a month, which gives him little chance to research the water, so he generally starts finding out what the fish will take by process of elimination; that is, he keeps changing flies until he hits pay dirt. This time he was lucky and took a limit on the Fledermouse and proved to himself, at least, that he could always make a reasonable catch on this nymph. Now he uses practically nothing else.

Another customer made a rather startling discovery about this nymph some five years ago while fishing for December steelhead on the lower Rogue River. The river was very low and clear and the fish spooky, especially of a boat. This particular run of fish were small in size compared to most winter fish, mostly in the six-pound range. It developed that when it came to the usual patterns of Rogue steelhead flies, the fish were not having any. Old standbys such as the Golden Demon, Juicy Bug, and Silver Hilton would not even get a flash. So as a last resort this angler went to nymphs. When he gave them a #8 Fledermouse, things began to happen fast and furious. For the rest of his three-day stay, he averaged five steelhead a day, and on the Rogue that is far above par.

Since that time, this customer (who is, in a way, a collector of my flies) buys the Fledermouse six dozen at a time. He has unlimited confidence in this nymph, and so do I.

Casual Dress Nymph

This nymph has been saved for the end of the series for just one reason. While the body is spun with the fur noodle, it is the only one where the fur is not prefelted; that is, mixed in a soapy bath. Instead, the noodle is made direct from the back of a heavily furred muskrat. It is usually tied on #4 or #6 3XL and 2XS hooks (#1206 by Wright & McGill). However, much like the Fledermouse and Hare's Ear, it will produce well on any size because it seems to be universally accepted by the fish, and not just trout. Tied on #2s and #4s for bass and #10s and #12s for panfish, it is a killer. Like several other patterns, its existence came about purely by accident.

In mid-October of 1960 two of us made a trip to the Upper Big Deschutes River where it enters Wick-i-up Reservoir in central Oregon. This being my first trip to this particular water, I did one of my usual tricks: I tied up a few of something new to try out. This something new happened to be three Casual Dress Nymphs.

Why the name? A look at the illustrated specimen should answer that without further question. Nothing could be more casually dressed—one might say "thrown at the hook" in the hope it would stick long enough to make a catch. But it was a tremendous success, as witnessed by the fact that, while we landed only four browns of two to four pounds, we shared in hooking six fish, all of which we were certain exceeded ten pounds. While so doing, we managed to lose all three nymphs, and we were using eight-pound tippets. The Casual Dress has been a standard production ever since and never fails to be worthy of anyone's fly book.

Tying the Casual Dress Nymph

Hook: For the purpose of the following instructions, it will be tied on the big #4 3XL and 2XS hook.
Tying Thread: Black.
Tail: A short, thick bunch of muskrat back fur with all guard hairs left in.
Body: Lay something like a shoebox lid in your lap. Cut off enough muskrat back fur to create a noodle three inches long, well tapered at the rear but as thick as a lead pencil in front. Now scramble this fur in the box lid until the guard hairs are pointing to all points of the compass. When thor-

oughly mixed, assemble it in a pile three inches long and one inch wide. It should have been mixed well enough to pick up and lay in the palm of your hand. It takes considerable dampness to roll this well, so I dip my fingertips in a saucer of water before rolling the fur. You must handle this a bit more carefully than you do the prefelted fur.

Use a spinning loop at least an inch longer than the noodle, leave an excess of room for a fur collar as you did for the Hare's Ear and Fledermouse. Spin the body and use plenty of cement under it. It may look ragged enough as it is, but I give it the old hacksaw treatment anyway so the guard hairs are feathered out like a centipede's legs. A fur collar of the same muskrat back fur should cover the front third of the body.

Head: A black ostrich head of four of the widest flues you have finishes it off.

No wing cases? They don't seem necessary on this one.

While it appears to represent some tidbit of very active food to the fish, it really simulates nothing more than just that—food. But to give you an idea how much we can be mistaken, I quote the following from the fish-eye view.

One of our local state aquatic biologists in a wet suit was diving and studying spawning redds here on the Williamson a year or so ago and a fly caster allowed a big #4 Casual Dress to drift over him. "Hey! What does that bug look like from underneath?" he asked the biologist.

"Looks like it had an air balloon around it," he answered. "Actually, it takes on the hazy appearance of a minnow, and does it have action. Everything is going for it."

Maybe we should all own a wet suit and do a bit more observance and research from the fish's end of the spectrum.

One last suggestion for the Casual Dress. You can tie it with the noodle of fur prefelted, but it will never be quite as casual in appearance as this version. It looks for all the world like a small drowned mouse, plus many other hazy simulations when well soaked. Inasmuch as a mouse makes top bait for all game fish, it may be that is how they identify it.

Ideas and Theories

What you have read up to now represents a fly tyer's life of research and trial-and-error methods, both in nymph tying as well as presentation, covering over forty-five years and bringing the history of the fuzzy nymphs up to the present. Along the way, I have adapted many of the newer synthetic materials to the fuzzy-nymph style, so I cannot be accused of being a stick-in-the-mud. I now present an argument in favor of the fuzzy nymphs as opposed to the exact imitations in lacquered bodies, molded rubber, latex, or plastic.

As stated earlier in this work, I was lucky enough to get started off on the right foot; lucky in not having available what had been written on the subject up to that time; also lucky enough to have the Willmarth and Young catalogs of materials.

It is true I dabbled with certain Humpys, Hardbacks, and related creations in later years but they didn't begin to compare with my own fuzzy creations when it came to producing strikes. One salient fact always remained: while the hardshells produced a few far-between strikes, few of these strikes were ever hooked solid. There had to be a concrete reason for this because the big percentage of strikes on the fuzzy nymphs were hooked and landed.

It took quite a while for the light to dawn on me, but when it did, I thought, "How stupid can one be?" As we all know, a fish rejects an artificial immediately on detecting it is a fraud, so it follows that biting down on a hard body makes the fraud that much more quickly detected—and rejected. Conversely, a soft body feels more like the natural, so it is held in the mouth that fraction of a second longer that allows for secure hooking. I find of late years my reaction time is not what it used to be; I need that extra fraction.

The second, and to me most important, reason for the high degree of success of the fuzzy nymphs brings together two important facts. To be consistently successful, a nymph must appear alive to the fish from any angle. When a fuzzy-bodied nymph is saturated and reaches the vision of the fish,

10

every filament on the body—tail, legs, even the wing cases—vibrates, and this is enhanced tenfold by short quick movements of the rod tip. Now try this with the hardshells, molded plastic, latex, and rubber versions. The body remains dead in the water! The only action is a bit from the legs and the tail.

Second, I am convinced that trout do not feed on dead nymphs. Dead or spent flies, yes, but nature seems to have given the trout definite guidelines. The dead or spent fly has completed its life cycle; the dead nymph has died an unnatural death and is not acceptable food.

It would appear that few, if any, of the researchers in the nymph field have delved much into the comparison in sizes among the different stages of aquatic insects; that is, the size of the adult in relation to the size of its nymph. I wrote an article devoted entirely to this subject a year or so ago, which was later published in *The Angler.* Apparently from a total lack of ripples—that is, no letter comment on it—it was not considered important.

No one seems to think it is important that a *Pteronarcys californica* nymph is always twenty percent larger than the adult, and as we drop down the scale in sizes, the disparity grows tremendously. When we reach the Diptera and the Chironomids, we find the larva a 3XL #14, the pupa a regular-length shank #12, and the adult a #18 or #20, but still we keep right on tying the pupae for this one on a #20 or #22 and then wonder why we have such lousy luck during a big tailing rise. Believe me, I left this tradition behind twenty-five years ago. What awakened me was a small sampling screen, an indispensable extra when scouting new waters, which allowed me to compare adults and nymphs. The lesson is obvious. Just for the hell of it, try tying one or two of your favorite larva, pupa, and nymph on a size larger or even two sizes larger hook and see what happens.

Equipment and Methods of Presentation

I am taking it for granted that if you have read this far and have put into practice my methods of nymph tying, you now have on hand a selection of finished nymphs. So, without further ado, let us learn something about using them.

This theme was touched on lightly here and there in the preceding chapters in a disconnected way. That will now be rectified. No more tying will be discussed, only methods of presentation, possible hours of best success, and last but certainly not least, proper tackle for nymphing.

Tackle

Proper tackle first: I have found it inadvisable to use just any old rod, reel, and line combination for what I consider a rather specialized field in angling. When fishing a dry fly, I prefer a very-fast-action rod, but this action does not work well for fishing nymphs. Too often the strike is soft (although it may also be quite deliberate)—seldom the flashing rise and sudden retreat that occurs when fishing dry.

After testing out every rod I have with various sizes of nymphs and on all types of creeks, rivers, and lakes, I finally decided that a slow-action rod with a full-length flex has the effect of anticipating the strike, hence more fish are hooked. The subtle takes of a bulging fish are easier to detect when the rod is easier to move or already flexed.

In just the past four or five years, sudden demand from more exacting anglers—those who want to have the best tool for nymphing—has almost revolutionized rod making. We now have available what I term full-flex or slow-action rods in bamboo, glass, and graphite. Being strictly a bamboo man, I have two of these, and just so no one will be able to accuse me of partisanship, I will only say they come from two of the world's top makers of fine bamboo rods. One of these is eight and one half feet in a very soft action that takes an 8 DT, either a floater or a wet tip. I use this rod exclusively when I am fishing a big #4 Stone Nymph. It also gets the job done when using a #4 or #6 Casual Dress or Fledermouse.

The other rod was originally a seven-and-one-half-foot dry-fly rod, but an ex-friend dropped a big tackle box on the tip, leaving the rod semiparabolic, and with a 6 DT line it performs beautifully. All in all, for nymphing these two are supreme; both are so sensitive one can almost feel the fish taste before it strikes.

As a kind of yardstick, it would seem that the length of the nymphing rod should be governed entirely by the type of water being fished. If you are wading deep, you may require an eight-and-a-half-footer in order to keep your backcast high enough, but when fishing from the bank on the smaller streams, I use a little wand of seven-foot three-inches and weighing three and three-fourths ounces.

Speaking of wading deep, or, say, casting with a cliff or trees close behind, this state of affairs has bred a new school of fly casters in only the last year or two. I refer to the superlight graphite rods, which one can wield in a ten-foot length weighing less than four ounces with a 7 line. These rods are used a lot on Oregon's steelhead rivers, which are bounded by rearward cliffs or timber, and in many of our lakes where wading out chest deep is the norm instead of the exception. These long superlight rods enable the caster to reach not only great distances, but to attain a consistently high backcast with none of the usual thing of the fly or nymph drowning behind him.

Lines

Considering lines, you actually need two: one a full-floater, the other a floater with a Sink-Tip. The Sink-Tip with ten feet of sinking tip is ideal for high spring runoffs, as well as when using the larger nymphs. On the smaller streams I prefer a floating line and there are many makes available.

Reels

Any reel you would use for general fly casting will do for

most nymph fishing, although on my first foray for the big Wick-i-up browns, I learned that just any old reel didn't fill the bill. Here I needed a minimum of one hundred fifty yards of backing behind a regular thirty-five-yard weight-forward fly line. But these are extreme cases, the exception rather than the rule.

Leaders

Again, leaders must be chosen to fit the occasion. I have never found it necessary to go to extremes, to extra-long leaders or super-fine tippets. For fishing the very large nymphs, such as #4 2XS and perhaps 3XL, I advise a heavy-butted fast-taper nylon leader of seven and a half feet, tapered to six- or eight-pound tippet. Why so heavy? You just cannot turn those big nymphs over on your forward cast on anything less than six pounds, and level leaders are absolutely out for this type of casting; they are much too soft and limber in the butt. Coupled with this is another good reason: the special nymph rods with their slow full-flex action tend to throw a very tight loop on both back and forward casts. If you are addicted to the light, overlong leaders and still want to use the big nymphs, you will be in constant trouble. You will spend as much time untying knots as you will in fishing. I had to learn this the hard way long ago.

One thing you do learn, though, if you would enjoy good casting, is to employ as high a backcast as is feasible at all times. This also helps to eliminate hooking your rod tip with your nymph on the forward cast. Oh! you don't do that? All I can say is that you must lead a charmed life. We all do it.

For casting the smaller nymphs—#8 or as small as you want to go—and still considering stream fishing, the seven-and-a-half-foot length is still best, though, of course, here you may go down to as fine a tippet as you desire. On a #8 nymph, I like a tippet of four pounds; on a #12, two and a half pounds. These pound-tests may stir up controversy because I know many anglers use leaders tapered to as fine as half a pound when fishing dry with the tiny midges. But I don't feel that such delicacies are necessary for nymphing.

For lake fishing the leader should be longer; nine feet is a good standard to go by. You generally have plenty of room for the backcast on lakes and can handle the longer leader better here than when casting in a restricted area such as a small brushy stream.

Nymphing Time

Now we consider the better fishing hours, as well as what seems to be the best type of weather for fishing. The single best time to fish nymphs, at least in my experience, is when the fish are bulging or tailing. This, of course, means a rather steady observation of the waters you fish. Few of us are lucky enough to be there always at the right time.

Certainly nymphs seem to have rather set emergence hours, which repeat year after year, species by species. This fact, if carefully observed over a period of time and just as carefully filed away in your memory, will serve you well on all future fishing trips.

Here in central Oregon the Black Drake mayfly begins emergence as early as June 1 and generally continues till July 1. This can vary as much as a week to ten days either way, depending on whether we have a cold late spring, or an early warm one. In 1976 they came very early, about May 25, but we were having the worst drought in the state's history so our streams were low and warm quite early.

The nymph becomes active about 10:00 A.M. standard time, providing the air temperature is about seventy degrees and the sun is shining. On cloudy days this may start an hour later and generally lasts till about 2:30 P.M. Early in the emergence, say the first week, few adults are seen during these hours. The nymphs just seem to be swimming about hither and yon and the fish will be bulging all over the place. So, this is the time to concentrate on nymphing techniques. About midafternoon this activity tapers off, and then just about sundown the big leap upward takes place. Suddenly the air is blue with the mating hatch and you have to decide quick whether to go dry and catch a lot of the smaller fish or stay with the nymph and concentrate on the big bulges for those old lunkers who are too lazy to go up for the adults. Things can get confusing at such times; no matter which method you use, you will probably always wish you had used the other one.

Now this late evening emergence does not hold true after the first week. I have seen sporadic spells of emergence in mid-June all during the day. When this happens, the nymph is relegated to the fly box and the dun comes into its own—but not for long, because suddenly there will come a spinner fall, and the fish appear to be nymphing again.

At least I would have sworn such was the case on the Upper Williamson some five years ago. I switched to my nymph pattern but nary a touch; in fact, after a few casts, I was putting the fish down till my fishing partner down the stream yelled at me, "They are taking the spent, wet!" And so they were, which is why a round half-dozen spents with all hackle clipped off under the thorax are always in my fly box. The same set of circumstances is bound to come up again sometime.

The Yellow Drake is generally most active from an hour before sunset till dusk. Oddly enough, the Black Drake may not hatch every day, and on these odd days is when the Yellow Drake, both nymph and dry, are at their best. As a rule, these two drakes emerge during the same period of the hatching season, and it being such a giant hatch—especially the Black Drake—one does not need a great variety of nymphs and flies on the stream. But one had better have a lot of *all* stages of these drakes when this hatch is on.

The big *bicolor* Leadwing may be around on your favorite fishing water, but unless you are a late sundown or dusk addict, you may not see it for years. There are never a great many on the water at any one time, so they may not seem important to the trout's food menu. But this giant mayfly must be in the porterhouse class when it comes to tastiness, because a big rainbow will dash several feet across the current to catch one lone adult. On rare occasions I have seen an adult floating downstream on a dark cloudy day, and then a well-presented dry will raise the biggest trout in the stream. This even goes for the old resident browns, and no smarter strain of trout ever lived. They have seen, and avoided, everything.

I start fishing the nymph a half hour before sundown, and sometimes continue till dusk. At other times, if I see a number of big fish after the adult, I switch and go dry. Every strike on this nymph or the dry is an adventure, because I can't remember ever taking a fish on them under two pounds.

The Nondescript simulates several of the mayfly nymphs and as these may spread over May, June, and July, it is more versatile than the general run of mayfly nymphs. As a consequence, if I decide to fish a Nondescript, I do not let the time of day deter me. As long as it is May, June, or July, it will produce strikes. During these months any large mayfly in the brown spectrum serves notice that it is Nondescript time. The only thing to consider is sizes and weights of hooks: heavy hooks for heavy fast water and regular weight for the slow, smoother flows.

The Big Yellow May, *Hexagenia limbata,* was thoroughly discussed in the earlier chapter on the tying of the nymph and spinner and little more will be added here except to stress that this burrower is by no means restricted to streams. Along Oregon's coast there are many large lowland lakes and all of them have tremendous hatches of this big t-bone. A coast fisherman once told me that he had seen hatches of Yellow Mays on Ten Mile Lake that would rival any Black Drake hatch and bass and perch went berserk feeding on the surface. Some of these bass reach ten pounds and fighting one on a fly rod and a Yellow May nymph or spinner could be a lot of sport.

The Yellow May Nymph however, with its colors and

overall bugginess, is so tasty in appearance that it will provoke strikes in or out of season. One or two fish are always willing to take a chance on it.

In all of my observations, I have never seen a green damsel nymph active before 10:00 A.M. or after 3:00 P.M. Apparently they need the hot sun to bring them to the stage of climbing up a reed or grass stem to hatch. This does not mean you can only take fish on a Green Damsel in the top strata of water—far from it. If nothing is moving on the surface, try one on a 2XS hook and a Sink-Tip line; ideal water would be ten or twelve feet in depth. Allow the nymph to settle all the way to the bottom, then retrieve in very short fast jerks.

Let me tell you another Green Damsel story. Two fishermen friends from Bend, Oregon, were fishing East Lake. One of these fellows puffs on a cigar most of the time. They had been fishing a Green Damsel Nymph in the film with no results. Then Henry had to lay his rod down to light up a fresh stogie. During the interlude, his rod lay in the boat and when he picked it up the old silk line and nymph were on the bottom.

Henry started a fast jerky retrieve and thought he was hung up. He was—on five pounds of fighting rainbow. They hooked and boated several more the same day using a new accidentally learned technique. So it would seem that mid-

May through September is all Green Damsel time.

An early spring and consequent warming of water temperatures will bring the dark stones, *Pteronarcys californica* into action. This also holds true of the golden stone, *catoneuria californica,* but inasmuch as the dark hatch starts in April on most streams in Oregon, the golden seldom appears before June 5. I think this is the earliest date I have recorded.

The dark stonefly hatch is generally well along by the time our trout season opens the last Saturday in April. Both of these big stones are midday hatches, so it has been determined that it is best to fish the nymph from 9:00 A.M. till 3:00 P.M. and then go to the big wet bucktail.

I fish both the nymph and the wet in the same manner: cast directly across stream, allow to drift and sink a foot or more on a Sink-Tip line, and then start agitating the rod tip with very short fast two-inch jerks.

I keep on using this same action throughout the drift, keeping the rod tip up at thirty degrees and always toward the nymph or fly, as the case may be. This action causes the entire surface of the nymph or fly to flow and appear to be alive, plus the action of the tail, legs, and wing cases. If your reactions are anywhere near par, you will miss few strikes with these methods. One thing you must never do: swim a nymph upstream against the slightest current. On a lake, yes, but never on a running stream. A nymph in the current is always swimming upstream, but at the same time he is going backward in the current.

The Little Yellow Stonefly, *Isoperla Marmona,* while having the same shape and many of the same habits of the two previously discussed insects, differs from them widely in other respects. Much smaller, #10 3XL, and of a chartreuse color, it first emerges in late June. but it has an extended hatch and occurs sporadically until early August. The adult may be observed on the wing on cloudy, sultry days, but the big hatch takes place about sundown and lasts till it is too dark to see them. This does not mean the nymph is not effective during midday. It is, even more so than late, because after sundown the trout tend to prefer the dry.

Fish the nymph as shallow as possible but still keep it submerged. After sundown when you start seeing a lot of dry rises is when the Little Yellow Stone female tied fore and aft with the crimson egg sac becomes queen of the river.

The Little Brown Stonefly, *Taeniopteryx pacifica,* also called the Little Red Stone, appears in April and its first emergence seems to coincide almost as if planned, about the time of the general opening of trout season. This is very much in favor of the fly fisherman because with the uncertain weather we have in late April, it's a toss-up whether to go fishing or watch television. But if you get two or three hours of warm sun during midday, both the Little Brown Stone nymph and dry will produce. Water temperatures seem to have little effect on their emergence time. Spring Creek's temperature will be forty degrees and northern California's Butte Creek sixty degrees, but still the Little Brown Stone will be present. I think we fail to appreciate its reliability, a rare trait in an aquatic insect. This little stone helps to fill in from season's start till sometimes as late as early July when there is no overlap of what we consider the more important fly hatches.

The light or Cinnamon Caddis, the Limnephiladae, seems to have no set emergence date. I find no set rule insofar as hours are concerned, nor is there any hard or fast rule on when they are in season. We have successive hatches of Light Caddis from April to November. They just vary a bit as to size and color, so I am liable to use any stage of its development at any time, with daylight or dusk preferred for the big wet bucktail or dry. The pupa seems at its best between 4:00 P.M. and sundown. This probably accounts for the reason a #6 or #8 Blonde Burlap or the same sizes in a tan shrimp are so effective.

The Dark Caddis, family Limnephiladae, genus *Dicosmoecus,* is much more consistent, both as to hours of activity as well as season. Seldom will you see a winged adult before the first of August, and rarely before sundown. That hour, just before dark, a Dark Caddis Pupa fished just under the surface right where a fish has just boiled is bound to put you where the action is.

This pupa swims freely to the surface after leaving the case, which makes it especially vulnerable to hungry fish. Of the three caddis pupa and larva presented, I consider it by long odds my favorite.

After being so closely associated for so many years with the Dark Caddis, it came as a distinct shock to learn there is an almost exact counterpart of the fall species that emerges in March. This does the angler no good because fishing is not legal till late April, but finding giant *Dicosmoecus* by the hundreds crawling all over the highway bridge abutments on Spring Creek in a hatch that to all appearances matched the August-to-November hatches was disconcerting to say the least. The only difference I could detect was in the coloration of the head: the fall hatch has a blackish head. The spring hatch have a medium burnt orange head the exact color of the body.

The Green Rockworm, Rhyacophiladae, is a simulation of the free-swimming caddis family. It would seem that only in the Far West do we have the right combination of water and habitat to produce several of the caddis genera that require #6 or even #4 hooks to get a correct correlation of size with the naturals.

This is the only caddis that I tie strictly as the larva. Actually, I doubt if a trout has much chance to capture one in the pupa stage, since when it goes into pupation it spins a protective net around itself in a crevice or between rocks, and all if have observed were quite close to the surface. So when it is ready to emerge it has only to climb a few inches to be out of reach of the trout and on the wing.

For these reasons, I fish the larva in rocky or shingle-bottom riffles, preferably three feet deep, upstream, on a wet-tip line, the sunny hours from 10:00 A.M. to 2:00 P.M. being the most productive. June, July, and August are all good months, as the adults appear intermittently over a considerable span of time.

The best time to fish a Muskrat Nymph is any time you can get to fishing water, be it stream or lake. Also, just about any hour of the day. A #8 or #10 simulates various stages of the cranefly larva and a #12 or #14 does the same for the black midge or mosquito larva. With all of these so predominant everywhere one can hardly miss.

Fishing hours for the Hare's Ear recall the wide latitude given to the Muskrat: most anytime, but still the best hours are very early and very late. And it cannot be overstressed that both the Black Midge Pupa and the Hare's Ear are at their best just barely submerged.

While the Black Midge pupa has the formation of a small Muskrat Nymph before pupation, you have much more latitude with the Muskrat. Not so the pupa: daylight until shortly after sunrise and sunset until dark are the limits.

One might lump the Blonde Burlap and the Freshwater Shrimp together. However, for some unexplained reason, a #8 shrimp is about as big as is really effective, whereas I use the Blonde Burlap as large as #2 with good success. It may be the Blonde is irresistible with that long blonde hackle (or hair) flowing around her. Hours mean nothing it seems, and neither does depth, though they probably ride rather deep on the heavy hooks and Sink-Tip line.

The same suggestions might well apply to the Casual Dress and Fledermouse. Anywhere, anytime, and under all conditions. These simulate only a general food source and their forte is in filling in the voids created by a lack of hatches. Even in streams and lakes abounding in shrimp there must be days when something new and edible-looking will produce to the exclusion of all the native food available.

It would be hard to say when *not* to use the Near Enough. It simulates so many mayfly nymphs swimming, sitting, clambering, and running that some one of the family is always available for a hungry trout. So I would say that, when in doubt, start off with a #8 Near Enough and work up to a #16 if necessary, or until you find which size produces, then just fish.

Presentation

Small-stream fishing will be considered first, streams where you will seldom use the big nymphs. Let us picture a winding meadow stream, deep, with now and then an undercut bank, first on one side and then on the other. It's too deep to wade, but narrow enough so that most of the undercuts on both sides can be well covered, as well as any likely feeding spots in midstream. This means a stream not over twenty or more feet in width. If it is wider, it is best to let your fishing pal fish the other bank because you will only scare the fish on the far side by dragging your line across the stream. Of course, if you are alone, try to find a crossing halfway through your day and fish the opposite bank coming back. Our local Wood River is exactly this type of stream: thirty feet wide and beautiful. I fish upstream a half mile, cross on a shoal, and then fish back.

Always sneak up on this kind of stream. Don't ever walk up and just start casting blindly. I am told they can't hear, but trout are certainly frightened by unusual vibrations carried through the stream's bank.

Assuming your rod is already set up and you are ready to fish, tread as lightly as possible in your approach to the bank. Try to make this approach at a place where there is no overhanging bank, but where it shelves off, if possible.

When you are in position to look upstream or down and study all the overhangs on your bank, do just that, looking for hiding places. This not only gives you a mind's-eye picture for reference, but, just as important, it allows time for all vibrations to dissipate and for any alarmed fish to settle down. If you are a fair-to-good dry-fly fisherman, you need none of this advice on a careful approach. You will have mastered this technique long ago.

I have found that on small nymphs you can cast either upstream or downstream and still have good success, though I would stress the necessity of what we call a slack-line cast when fishing downstream along the near bank. This is accomplished by a sudden sharp lift of the rod tip just before the nymph touches the water. This causes the line to jerk back, and allows the leader and a few feet of line to drop on the water in loose curves. This type of cast gives the nymph time to submerge and drift a few feet before drag sets in. When the drag first becomes apparent, feed the line through the guides at the rate the stream is flowing or even a mite

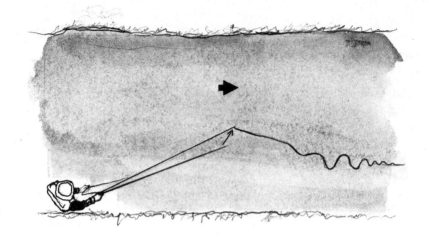

slower. A waiting fish will take to thinking that the nymph is making a struggle to best the current and isn't quite making it. Tactically, this also gives you the advantage of drifting your nymph into places where it could not be cast. I have often fed out as much as ten feet of extra line in this manner in order to reach otherwise unfishable areas, such as under overhanging willows, grass, and such.

In lake waters and slow-moving streams a fully developed nymph can swim very fast and even gain a bit upstream against a slow current, especially the damsels. Consequently, creating a bit of drag while agitating the rod tip will often bring a smashing strike when otherwise the fish might let it pass on by. Browns are real nasty about this; they often have to be teased into thinking a big hatch is in the making.

When I find a long stretch of overhanging bank and I am certain there must be one or more good fish under it, I may drop my nymph down in successive stops and drifts as many as a dozen times. I have had a fish flash under it on the first cast and hook it on the tenth. But when doing this, you must not make even one tiny mistake or you'll put the fish down for at least ten minutes.

Some years ago I was fishing on the headwaters of the Williamson River with a Black Drake Nymph. This river is identical in size and flow with the one we have been discussing: twenty feet wide, very deep with a slow, smooth current, lots of overhanging banks only six inches above the water. Time, 11:00 A.M., and the trout were bulging on the surface everywhere. My first cast brought an explosion: a sixteen-inch rainbow arced out from under the bank and went completely over it without touching it. It made such a splash on landing that it put down two smaller fish feeding ten and twenty feet downstream. Something was wrong with my presentation, but to this day I haven't figured out the answer.

Nothing can be done about this but go away and come back later—give the fish a good rest and the next time, knowing just where it will be, try to correct your previous fault. I proceeded to catch several nice trout upstream and two hours later I came back all prepared to catch that acrobat. I did too, but it wasn't really authentic.

There didn't seem to be any change of technique advisable; in fact, my first presentation still seemed the best possible. So I aimed my cast to drop the nymph about six inches in front of its nose. He did the same thing as on the first cast—arced completely over the nymph—but this time I was ready for it and snagged him under the chin, or where a fish's chin would be if it had one. I was so keyed up that my reflexes went off automatically when it broke water, and the nymph was in the right place at the right time.

If you have ever snagged a prime fish of any size and on light tackle, you know what a fight that rainbow gave me: six jumps in as many different directions with hardly a pause in between. Then it tried to hide under the bank, probably hoping to find an old beaver den, but I managed to get the fish out in midstream again, and the last aerial try was so close I could see where it was hooked. This prompted me to become very cautious, because a snagged fish does not lead too well and all can be lost at the last moment. But this fish was not meant to escape and I certainly didn't want a broken leader, so slow and easy was the only way. Suffice it to say I got my nymph back and if someone else hasn't taken him, he may still be right under that same overhang. Should weigh about eight pounds by now.

Turning to upstream technique, I used two methods. On the first I try to cast a few feet above where the overhang or

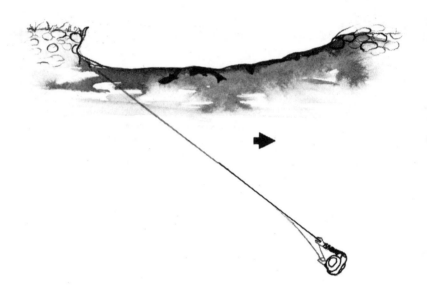

undercut begins so that any small splash will not put a fish down. The nymph should not be more than a few inches deep on its drift back to you. This enables you to see both the nymph and the flash of the fish. Strike! Never fail to do so, because some of the old lunkers will simply drift out from under the bank, engulf the nymph, and just as sneaky-like drift back to their lairs.

Almost invariably a striking fish will flash out in a curve, take the nymph, and go back to his retreat, though it is true you at times have to create what it thinks is the start of a hatch. In this case the fish may take a look on the first cast and be taken on the tenth. Trout are much easier hooked when fishing a nymph shallow upstream because you pull the hook into it instead of away from it as you do in a downstream drift.

The second method, used casting straight upstream, is the one I employed forty-five years ago when I cast my first nymph. Make the cast so the nymph drops just barely on the bank and, with a twitch of the rod tip, cause it to roll into the water. This is not advisable if the bank is high (that is, over a foot) because too much splash results. And it is not a good idea to roll it in right over a fish; try to do it at least three feet upstream from where you anticipate a strike. Be sure you are ready for instant action; I break more tippets this way—too keyed up, the fish is an old lunker, or I'm using a pound-and-a-half tippet. But it's all fun, and after all, that is mainly what I am after.

Fishing the far bank is mainly an upstream presentation. Downstream, unless the stream is very narrow, you can't get away from instant drag. On big fast water, drag is not too important, but on slow water and small streams it doesn't produce many strikes.

When fishing the far banks, dropping the nymph on the edge of the bank and flipping it into the water has its positive advantages. It also has one big disadvantage: you lose a few nymphs that way. They hang up in the grass and you part a tippet trying to retrieve them. But who cares; you're tying your own now and two cents isn't enough to cause you to wade the stream, let alone fill your waders and put down a good fish. Break it off and tie on another one. The fish are feeding and time is of the essence.

The positive advantage of this case is that it almost completely eliminates the chance of scaring the fish, since you should have dropped it several feet upstream from any expected rise. When it is flipped into the water and drifts two or three feet, it is at the right depth when it reaches the vision of the fish.

Don't expect to achieve a long drift casting up and across to the far bank. The only logical way this can be done is if the current is fast under the far bank, slowing down gradually back toward your side. This state of affairs tends to compensate for drag and will give you a few more feet of drift.

A second advantage in dropping the nymph on the far bank may come to you this way: you've made the cast, and just before you flip it out onto the water, a fish bulges right under it. Try to retrieve it without it touching the water. On narrow streams this is easy. On wide ones, go ahead and drop it in his face; you may be lucky. But it is best to make another cast several feet upstream and flip it in—this decreases the chances of scaring him.

If you have a sensitive rod and can drop a #10 dry fly without a ripple, go ahead and use your regular casting technique. Just try to make your leader straighten out not more than two or three inches above the water. A #10 nymph does not have the balloon-like buoyancy of a like-size dry fly, and it drops faster, with more splash. But practice will make a sharpshooter out of you and be a big help when you are using the dry fly.

Still speaking of small streams, most mountain creeks are fast brawling water, though they may slow down in meadow stretches at times. These waters require a downstream approach under most conditions. As a consequence, I fish a nymph here almost the same way I would fish a small wet fly. An all-floater line will suffice for all your needs, unless there are abnormally deep runs where a Sink-Tip might be an advantage. Just remember: never swim the nymph against the current. Natural nymphs have enough trouble bucking the flow in a meadow stream, let alone a racing riffle. Just cast across current and follow the nymph with rod tip up about thirty degrees from the horizontal and keep the tip vibrating the full drift. You seldom catch big fish in such waters, but eight-to-ten-inchers are best in the frying pan anyway.

In the second edition of *Fuzzy Nymphs,* I bemoaned the fact that I had moved some six miles away from my favorite river. Well, I am back now, but sad to say that on the last five miles before it enters Upper Klamath Lake and on the last six miles of the Williamson there is no fly water per se. It's all very deep, slow trolling water, so I can't look out the back window and know by a bit of observation if it is time to go fishing or not. But I haven't forgotten that June 21, 1960, and the sudden impromptu fishing it afforded. It was one of those that one never forgets.

I had been uptown to the post office, and on my return at 11:00 A.M. I glanced out the window and saw a big tail break the surface of the slick water with a splash that could be seen a full hundred yards away. There was a stack of fly orders on the desk, all overdue, but someone else would have to do them now. I was going fishing.

I was in such a hurry to get going that I nearly forgot to put the perishable groceries in the icebox. There was no question about what to use: Golden Stoneflies were crawling all over the house walls. Some were even in the house. Now fish were tailing all over the river. In the slicks, fast or slow water, they were gorging themselves on a tremendous rush of nymphs.

It was almost too easy. My big problem that morning was stopping those wild leaping rainbows. Somehow every one hooked seemed to be wilder than the one before. I don't know how long I spent battling those big rainbows, probably two hours, and I seldom had to make more than two or three casts between strikes. The rest of the time I spent trying to land them. I had a big morning, nine fish on and five landed, and while I weighed only one that scaled five pounds as a keeper, they all ran three to six pounds, and I am certain I lost one of eight or more.

For the big nymphs like the Golden Stone, the approach and casting technique is essentially steelhead-type fishing. Again I stress the use of heavy leaders, not only so big fish will not break off on the strike, but because you just can't turn those big #4, 3XL nymphs over on the forward cast with a wispy leader. Half the time the nymph hits the water and line, tip, and leader top keep on going. It's a perfect way to tie the Gordian knot in your tippet, or even your line.

Then again I have lost too many fish on a six-pound tippet to trust them any more. The break-off is invariably on the strike; if I can get the hook into the fish without the leader parting, I can generally land him; it's that sudden shock of the strike that does the damage.

In heavy water, cast directly across the stream; allow time for the nymph to sink a foot: a ten-foot drift should do it. Keep the rod tip up thirty degrees above the horizontal

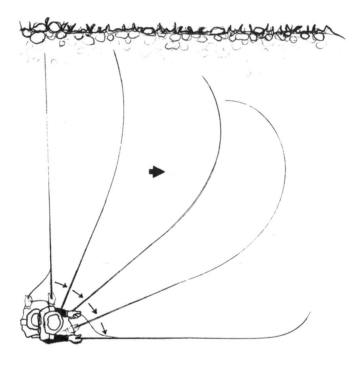

and follow the line with the rod. Never keep the rod pointed across the current. This is a sure way to put a set in a rod; it's also a good way to miss strikes. With the rod in one hand, I always have the line in the other, and when after fish that may exceed five pounds, I want ten feet of loose line between my hand and the reel. A ten-pound fish going away on the strike will often overrun the best reel, and the loose line gives you a fighting chance to meet that first wild rush.

The nymph is worked constantly along the full arc of the drift. Very short, choppy jerks imparted to the tip by both the rod hand and the other on the line work best for me. I started out over fifty years ago using only one hand; I used the other only when winding the reel. I also lost a lot of fish that way until an angler of long experience showed me how to fish with both hands.

Of course, I still lose fish. In steelheading you may expect most of your strikes on the forty-five-degree angle downstream. This is easy to account for, because at this point the nymph has reached its greatest depth. The pull of the current starts it rising to the surface, though with the sinking tip this will not be quite so pronounced as with a floater.

This rising of the nymph to the surface imitates what the natural does during emergence, so it is only logical to expect the strike at this time. A fish may have been following it, undecided as to whether it is the real thing or not, but when it starts to the surface it loses all doubt and takes it. These are vicious strikes because it is already headed across and downstream, so when the fish feels the steel he opens all afterburners, contributing to twice as much shock as the average strike.

Up until eight years ago I had done little nymph fishing in Oregon's numerous lakes. Too many streams handy, and they are always my first love. Knowing, however, that I was going to need more experience in this field, I have made it a must not only to store up all the knowledge I could through my own efforts, but also to quiz every angler I could who fished nymphs in our lake waters.

To mention just a few of the larger ones where nymphs are most effective: Diamond, Elk, Davis, Wick-i-up Reservoir, Summit, Crescent, East, Paulina, and last but in a very special category, little Hosmer, where you fish Atlantic salmon for fun (fly only and barbless hooks). No fish may be killed unless you take a brook trout; these may be kept. Nearly all of these waters contain myriad shrimp and various caddisflies, so the stage is set for the Freshwater Shrimp and Dark Caddis Pupa.

Davis Lake is especially productive for big rainbow and coho salmon, and those five-pound coho dote on a big #6 Muskrat or a like size of the Green Damsel. Lake fishing is truly where the Green Damsel comes into its own. It is good June until October on all of the aforementioned lakes, plus dozens of others too numerous to mention.

Here is where you go to a nine-foot leader, and as you will rarely use anything larger than a regular-weight #8 3XL, you can probably go as fine on tippets as desired. On lines you could find a use for three, and all in one day's fishing.

Remember the episode mentioned earlier where my friends from Bend accidentally let one sink to the bottom with such good results. If Henry had had a H-DWT, he might not have landed more fish, but he would certainly have gotten down to them a lot faster. Then there are times when a slow sinker would be best. I know a fellow who trolls a Black Drake Nymph with a slow sinker when fishing in Diamond Lake. He says it gets the nymph down about two feet and that depth produces all the strikes. With this line, you could do the same thing casting and use a slow, jerky retrieve.

Personally, I prefer a full floater for lake fishing, because I like to drift my boat about fifty feet from the reed beds and cast just ahead of a bulging fish. How do I know which way he is traveling? Wait for the second bulge. It's a dead giveaway and he seldom reverses direction unless alarmed, and then you won't catch him anyway.

Davis Lake has some of the greatest Green Damsel hatches imaginable. The rainbow here reach fifteen pounds; the coho salmon sometimes ten, and the Atlantics as much or more.

Some odd things occur here over the average season. Coho may be going nymph crazy, while those giant rainbows want #16 Blue Quills dry, coupled with the Atlantics preferring a big yellow, white, and silver streamer. One can really get fouled up and frustrated with only one outfit. I wouldn't even consider going fishing on Davis without a minimum of three rods, lines and reels to match, and then I would very likely run into a situation where I needed another one. But don't we all?

In retrospect, looking back over fifty-six years of trout fishing and fifty years of fly tying, it is quite evident that a great volume of water has flowed under the bridge. Not only have there been great advances in all fields of the technology of fly tying, but a host of new highly adaptable tools are available—tools to fit any pocketbook if one must consider price. Also a galaxy unending of new fly-tying materials that would fill a small book just to describe.

Conservation of our rivers is now a living thing and the results are nothing less than beautiful. More and more streams are being added to the Wild Rivers category in order to perpetuate existing wild native stocks where no hatchery plants will ever be made. We came so terribly close to losing some of these wild native strains that we know now that these present programs should have been started twenty years ago. God grant it may ever be thus.

Afterword

This last chapter might be entitled a hodgepodge of new ideas and theories, a few fantasies, and the debunking of some myths that should be stricken from the record. There will also be a lot of new materials evaluated and passed on as good or bad.

Let's consider photo-dyed feathers first. With light oak turkey feathers almost a thing of the past, and if found, retailing for $2.50 to $3.50 for a matched pair, it becomes almost a necessity to use the photo-dyed jobs. Frankly, I don't like them, but I have to use them for my wet and dry grasshoppers; however, they leave out a lot to the appearance of the finished fly. I think they could do a much better job at mottling: finer mottling, more brown against a paler yellow background, and so on.

You later tyers won't believe this, I know, but nearly twenty years ago I bought two pounds of rights and lefts of Pennsylvania wild turkey, all light oak, for $2.50 a pound. I bought them from H. J. Noll of Doylestown, Pennsylvania, before Pennsylvania banned all export of wild turkey feathers from the state. Shades of yesteryear!

A host of new dubbing materials have appeared on the market in the last few years and the variety is still expanding. Almost all of this is good for spinning my fuzzy bodies. Most are imitation seal and may be short or long fiber, so choose which you like to work with best.

If I can find a blend of, say, three or more colors that add up to the color I want, this is the one I buy, and for this reason: If you will put a 10X glass over most nymphs, even the adults, you will observe that several shades of the basic color make up the whole, hence the blend of colors of my body materials. For instance, the yarn I use to tie my Green Damsel Nymph is a light greenish olive, but if you examine it closely, you will find three shades of green and two of yellow. When wet, it copies the nymph *Calopteryx yakima* to perfection. And this genus is prevalent all over the West.

Coming back to the various dubbing materials, I would not advise trying to blend several colors of the long-fiber kind. It would be feasible in a dishpan, but definitely not in the Wife's blender—you wind up with a knotted ball around the spindle. It can be a problem to untangle. Stick with the medium and short material. A blend of these two lengths strengthens the desired end product.

Not enough use is made of burlap in the tying of nymphs. Several years ago, several of the editors of the fly-tying sections of our fly-fishing magazines were crying for some body material that would recreate the air-bubble sheath on emerging caddis pupae. They finally got happy when Sparkle yarn and Dazzle-Aire came on the market, but a well roughed-up burlap body does a much better job. Every filament end carries a minute air bubble. That is the main reason why my Blonde Burlap will outfish a Shrimp or Scud simulation, and they both simulate the same crustaceans. Perhaps I should skip the yarn on the Shrimp and tie both out of burlap. Just this past year I have gone entirely to burlap for my Green Rockworm bodies, and with pronounced success. The tiny bubbles do it. Top-quality burlap is available by the yard or less in all good fabric stores and you have a host of colors to choose from. Dirt cheap, too.

Where once we were limited to wool or silk for fly bodies, we now can go crazy in a Super Yarn Mart with every known synthetic, plus a host of blends containing nylon, Orlon, Banlon, polypropylene, and mohair blends, till one gets confused and dizzy trying to decide what to try next.

Ten years ago there was a big Super Yarn Mart in Medford, Oregon. It was a good thing it was eighty miles over the Cascade Divide or that galaxy of yarns would have kept me broke. I never got out of there without leaving a ten-dollar bill. As a result, I still have a big clothes closet in my tying room full of skeins of yarn I haven't even looked at for five years. All this stopped when there weren't enough women knitters in the Rogue Valley to support the store and they closed out. A good thing for me, too. I've saved a lot of money by it.

Now we come to some don'ts. I said at the beginning there would be some excoriating phrases regarding materials, fly designs, hooks being pushed on us we don't need, in fact, a lot of stuff just marketed to get our dollars.

One of the last columns the late Ted Trueblood wrote for *Field & Stream* was on the comparative values of the popular humpback type of shrimp and scud patterns tied on the English bait hooks, with, say, a regular Mustad 3906 #8, #10, or #12. Ted was a bit skeptical of their value, so instead of wasting four dollars for 100 hooks, he went out to the right lake habitat and seined some live shrimp. As usual, they curled up in his hand, but when released in his aquarium they immediately straightened out and swam in a straight line like a minnow until the guppies caught the last one. End of experiment. Ted bought no humpy hooks. After all, he was catching plenty of fish on the 3906.

A local friend several years later, though, had to do it the hard way. Knowing I would not stock the hooks, he bought a box and tied up a half dozen of our tan shrimp. He had been having better-than-average success on a 3906 #8 and could hardly believe it when his catch fell off fifty percent the first time out. This drop was not only in less strikes, but just as much in missed strikes. After three evenings of this, he went back to the 3906 and, presto! he was back in business.

Being a thorough researcher, in a couple of days he tried the humpies again. Same old story. The next time he saw me, he said, "Wanna buy some English bait hooks?" No way; I think he tossed them in the river.

The foregoing applies not only to shrimp and scud, but to all the caddis larvae and pupae. Pull a big caddis larva out of its case and lay it in the palm of your hand. It will curl up in a ball. Lay it in the water. It will sink and extend itself on the way to the bottom. Once there, it stays fully extended and starts crawling along the bottom, but always fully extended.

In his book of many years ago, *Aquatic Insects of California,* the late Dr. Paul Needham called the big dark stonefly *Pteronarcys californica* the Leaf Roller because it rolled up in a ball when in the hand. He apparently assumed it stayed thus when released in the water. Nothing could be further from the truth. When released, this big nymph straightens out in a flash and darts like a minnow to the bottom and under the first rock or into the first crack it finds to hide. So much for any kinked shanked hooks of any kind, including the big humpbacked stone nymphs. They never occur in that form.

The pronounced use of stiff tails of any kind, for instance goose biots, should be discouraged in the tying of nymphs. This also includes the use of extended bodies. Nothing stiff should extend beyond the curve of the hook. Why? Stiff tails and extended bodies stab the fish in the nose and you feel only a bump. There is never any meat on the hook. Admittedly, if the fish are three pounds and up their mouths will engulf the fly and the strike will be solid, with a hooked fish. But where is such fishing? Nowhere. Many more are taken where the average is under twelve inches, and the fish that can engulf the stiff tails and extended bodies are a rarity or nonexistent.

Now a word on the plastic body materials such as nylon, Swannundaze, raffia, and so on. Except for backcaps on nymphs and possibly wing cases, leave them alone. And if you do use any of these slick body materials on top of a nymph be sure the belly and thorax are plenty roughed up with the old hacksaw blade.

The latter part of this chapter should be caustic enough to start you thinking about your past experiences. I've no doubt murdered some pet beliefs and that was intended—I make no apologies. I want to start you thinking, to do more examining of facts.

Index

Acrylics, dyeing, 39, 40
American March Brown
   tying the, 116–20
   tying the Dun and Spinner
     versions, 120–21
Amphipoda. See Freshwater
   shrimp and scuds
Angler, The, 154
Aniline dyes, 40
Anopheles, 129, 130
Aquatic Insects of California, 183
Arana, Arnold, 141

Big Yellow May, 91
   description of, 102–103
   when to fish, 162–163
Big Yellow May Nymph
   tying the, 103–104
   tying, spinner, 104, 106
Black Drake, 94
   description of, 107–8
   when to fish, 160–61
Black Drake Dun, tying the spinner
   and spent versions, 110–12
Black Drake Nymph, 18–19, 40
   blending of fur for, 43–45
   tying the, 108–10
Black midge. *See* Midges
Bleaching techniques, 45–47
Blending of furs, 43–45
Blonde Burlap
   description of, 141
   tying the, 141–43
   when to fish, 168
Burlap, 182
Buz's Fly Shop, 55, 116

Caddis and the Angler, The, 84, 85
Caddisflies. *See under type of*
Caddis larva, simulation of, 16
Calineuria californica, 53–63
Calopteryx yakima, 87–89
Casual Dress Nymph
   description of, 149–50
   tying the, 150–51
   when to fish, 168
Catoneuria californica, 164
Chase, Jim, 115
Chironomus larva, 125–28
Cranefly, simulation of gray, 24

Damselfly
   simulation of, 19–20
   See also Green Damsel
Dark Caddis Emergent
   description of, 74–75
   when to fish, 166
Dark Caddis Emergent Nymph
   tying the, 75–77
   tying the adult, dry version, 80
   tying the adult, wet version,
     77–79
Dark Salmon Fly, 41, 49
Dark Stonefly, 41, 183–84
   description of, 49–50
   when to fish, 164–65
Dark Stone Nymph
   tying the, 50–51
   tying the adult, wet version,
     52–53
Dicosmoecus, 166–67
Diptera. See Midges
Doroneuria baumanni, 53–63

Dubbing
  creating, 21–23
  Fledermouse, 45
  materials, 181–182
Dyeing
  checking colors, 38–39
  creating black, 40
  creating brown, 41
  creating ginger, 39
  creating gold, 42–43
  creating lemon-barred, 37–38
  creating red, yellow, and orange, 41–42
  Ferezal, 37
  ostrich plumes, 40–41
  picric acid, 41–42
  setting colors, 39
  synthetics, 39–40
  utensils for, 36
Dyes
  aniline, 40
  type of, 36–37, 41

Ephemerella excrucians, 120
Ephemeroptera. See Mayflies

Fall Caddis, 79
Ferezal, 37
Field & Stream, 147, 183
Fledermaus, 145
Fledermouse dubbing, 45
Fledermouse Nymph
  description of, 146–47
  tying the, 147–49
  when to fish, 168
Floss skeins, use of, 20–21
Flyfisher's Entomology, 63
Freshwater shrimp and scuds
  simulation of, 18
  tying the, 133, 138
  when to fish, 168
Fuzzy nymph
  creation of first, 15–16
  versus exact imitations, 153–55
  when fish prefer, 17–18

Ginger hackle, imitating, 39
Golden Stonefly, 42
  classifications of, 54
  emergence of, 54–55
  when to fish, 164–65
Golden Stonefly Nymph
  tying the, 55–57
  tying the adult, dry version, 62–63
  tying the adult, wet version, 57–61
Great Leadwing Drake
  description of, 95–98
  when to fish, 161–62
Great Leadwing Drake Nymph
  tying the, 98–99
  tying the, dry version, 99–102
Great Western Leadwing, description of, 91
Great Western Leadwing Nymph, tying the 92–95
Green Damsel
  description of, 87
  when to fish, 163–64
Green Damsel Nymph, 19–20
  tying the, 87–88
  tying the, wet version, 88–89
Green Rockworm larva
  description of, 71–72
  when to fish, 167
Green Rockworm Nymph
  tying the, 72–73
  tying the adult, dry version, 74
  tying the adult, wet version, 73–74
Green Sedge, 71

Hackle tail, 19, 39
Hare's Ear Nymph
  description of, 143–45
  tying the, 145–46
  when to fish, 167–68
Herter dyes, 41
Hewitt, Edward R., 14, 72
Hexagenia limbata, 91, 102–106, 162
Hooks
  1XF, 66, 74, 84, 93, 110, 114, 121, 126
  1XL, 74, 75, 83, 84, 111, 114, 121, 141
  1XLF, 100
  2XS, 26, 50, 55, 64, 72, 77, 83, 116, 120, 141, 148, 149, 150

3XL, 26, 50, 55, 64, 65, 67, 69,
  72, 77, 80, 87, 89, 91, 94, 98,
  103, 104, 108, 113, 116, 122,
  131, 147, 148, 149, 150
4XL, 50, 93, 103
10XL, 66
humpy, 183
kinked shank, 184
by Mustad, 62, 65, 67, 69, 75,
  80, 83, 87, 89, 98, 104, 108,
  113, 122, 126, 133, 145
stiff tails, 184
by Wright & McGill, 55, 66, 74,
  84, 111, 114, 116, 121, 149

Isonychia bicolor, 97–102
Isonychia campestris, 122
Isonychia velma, 39, 91–95
Isoperla marmona, 63–67, 165

Kyte, Al, 53–54

Leaders, 159–60
Leisenring, Jim, 138
Leiser, Eric, 84
Lemon-barred wood duck,
  imitating, 37–38
Light Caddis Emergent
  description of, 80–81
  when to fish, 166
Light Caddis Emergent Nymph
  tying the, 81–82
  tying the adult, dry version,
    83–85
  tying the adult, wet version,
    82–83
Limnephilidae, 74–85, 166
Lines, 156
Little Brown Stonefly
  description of, 67
  when to fish, 165–66
Little Brown Stone Nymph
  tying the, 67–69
  tying the, dry version, 69
Little Yellow Stonefly
  locations for, 63
  when to fish, 165
Little Yellow Stone Nymph
  tying the, 64–65

tying female, dry version, 66–67
tying female, wet version, 65

McClane, Al, 147
McNeese, Dave, 84
March Brown. *See* American March
  Brown
Mayflies
  description of Near Enough
    Nymph, 121–22
  description of Nondescript
    Nymph, 115–16
  tying the Near Enough Nymph,
    122–23
  tying the Nondescript Nymph,
    116–20
  See also under type of
Microcaddis, 85
Midges, 155
  description of black, 125–26
  description of red, 128–29
  description of tan, 129–30
  simulation of black, 24
  tying the black midge pupa,
    126–28
  tying the tan midge pupa, 130
  when to fish, 168
Mosquito larva, 130–31
Muskrat Nymph
  blending of fur for, 43–45
  scoring of, 32
  sizes of, 24
  spinning of, 24–25
  tying the, 26–33
  when to fish, 167

Near Enough Nymph, 91
  description of, 121–22
  tying the, 122–23
Needham, Paul, 183
Nondescript Nymph
  description of, 115–16
  tying the, 116–20
  when to fish, 162
Noodle
  definition of, 15
  how to make a, 23–24

Odonata. See Green Damsel

Olson, Dee, 128
Ostrich plumes, 40–41

Photo-dyed feathers, 181
Picric acid, 41–42
Plastic body materials, 184
Plecoptera. See under type of Stonefly
Presentation
  downstream technique, 174
  in heavy water, 176–77
  in lake waters and slow-moving streams, 170–72, 177–79
  in small streams, 168–70
  upstream technique, 172–74
Pteronarcys californica, 49–53, 155, 164, 183–84
Pteronarcys dorsata, 49
Putnam Company, 37
Puyans, Andre, 94

Red midge. *See* Midges
Red Quill, 120
Red Stonefly. *See* Little Brown Stonefly
Red Upright, 120
Reels, 158–59
Rhyacophila grandis, 71–74, 167
Rit Company, 36
Rock sprawlers, 115
Ronald, Alfred, 63

Saddle hackle, 39
Schweibert, Ernie, 81, 92
Siphlonurus occidentalis, 94, 107–12, 122
Skues, G. E. M., 72
Snyder, Jack, 147
Solomon, Larry, 84
Spinnerin Yarn Co., Inc., 68
Stenonema vicarium, 116–21
Stone clingers, 115
Stoneflies. *See under type of*

Tackle, 157–58
Taeniopteryx pacifica, 67–69, 165–66
Tan midge. *See* Midges

Trichoptera. See under type of Caddisfly
Trout and Salmon Fisherman, A, 14
Trueblood, Ted, 183
Tying the Wet Fly, 138

Willmarth Company, 14
Wulff, Lee, 99

Yarns
  for American March Brown, 116
  for Big Yellow May, 103, 104
  for Black Drake, 108, 111
  for Black Midge Pupa, 126
  for Blonde Burlap, 141–42
  for Dark Caddis Emergent, 75, 78, 80
  Dazzle-Aire, 50–51, 82, 103, 104, 113, 182
  for Fledermouse, 148
  for Freshwater Shrimp, 133
  for Golden Stone, 56, 62
  for Great Leadwing Drake, 98
  for Great Western Leadwing, 93
  for Green Damsel, 87, 88, 89
  for Green Rockworm, 73, 74
  for Light Caddis Emergent, 82, 83
  for Little Brown Stonefly, 68
  for Little Yellow Stonefly, 64
  for Mosquito Larva, 131
  for Red Midge Pupa, 129
  for Tan Midge Pupa, 130
  types of, 181–82
  for Yellow Drake, 113
Yellow Drake
  description of, 112–13
  when to fish, 161
Yellow Drake Nymph, tying the, 113
Yellow Drake Spinner, tying the, 113–15
Yellow May. *See* Big Yellow May
Young, Paul, 14

Zygoptera. See Green Damsel